W9-AMN-376

The Standard
Carnival Glass
Price Guide

Revised 9th Edition

Bill Edwards

This comprehensive price guide is provided free with the purchase of
The Standard Encyclopedia of Carnival Glass,
or may be purchased separately for $9.95.

COLLECTOR BOOKS
A Division of Schroeder Publishing Co., Inc.

Searching For A Publisher?

We are always looking for knowledgeable people considered to be experts within their fields. If you feel that there is a real need for a book on your collectible subject and have a large comprehensive collection, contact us.

COLLECTOR BOOKS
P.O. Box 3009
Paducah, Kentucky 42002-3009

On The Cover:

Top Left: Loganberry, 10" tall, base diameter 3¾", four marks, made by Imperial, amethyst. See price guide.

Top Right: Wild Strawberry, 9" bowl, made by Northwood, amethyst. See price guide.

Bottom: Jewels, unpatterned iridized glass, made by Dugan, green candle bowl. See price guide.

Additional copies of this book may be ordered from:

Collector Books
P.O. Box 3009
Paducah, Kentucky 42002-3009

@$9.95. Add $2.00 for postage and handling.

Copyright: Bill Edwards, 1994

This book or any part thereof may not be reproduced without the written consent of the Author and Publisher.

Printed by IMAGE GRAPHICS, INC., Paducah, Kentucky

Color Code

M—Marigold
A—Amethyst or Purple
B—Blue
G—Green
PO—Peach Opalescent
AO—Aqua Opalescent
BO—Blue Opalescent
IG—Ice Green
IB—Ice Blue
SM—Smoke
CL—Clear
CM—Clambroth
V—Vaseline
R—Red
Pas—Pastel
AQ—Aqua
AM—Amber
IM—Iridized Moonstone
HO—Horehound
RenB—Renniger Blue
PH—Pastel Horehound
HA—Honey Amber
CT—Citrene
EB—Electric Blue
EmG—Emerald Green

PL—Pearl Opalescent
AB—Amberina
RA—Reverse Amberina
LV—Lavender
IC—Iridized Custard
VO—Vaseline Opalescent
PM—Pastel Marigold
W—White
TL—Teal
PeB—Persian Blue
CeB—Celeste Blue
AP—Apricot
BA—Black Amethyst
LG—Lime Green
RG—Russet Green (olive)
PK—Pink
MO—Milkglass Opalescent
LO—Lime Opalescent
RS—Red Slag
WS—Wisteria
CHP—Champagne
NG—Nile Green
MC—Marigold Custard
SMG—Smoke Milkglass

* Denotes a speculative price for an item that is rare and hasn't been on the market recently.

Note: While many prices have had an explosion of growth, especially on Northwood plates, red carnival and pastels, certain items after many years of growth have declined slightly or have remained constant. This price guide reflects these changes as well as is possible with today's ever-changing market. Please remember it takes months to print a price guide such as this, and in that time carnival glass sales do not remain static. While I have tried to allow for this passage of time from compilation to print, I cannot guess the future. Still, with over 33,000 price listings, this remains the most complete price source for carnival glass in the world, and I'm proud of the results.

Acorn Burrs

Apple Blossom Twigs

Apple Tree

Art Deco

	M	A	G	B	PO	AO	Pas	R
ACANTHUS (IMPERIAL)								
Bowl, 8"-9½"	65	90	110	90			75SM	
Plate, 10"	200						275SM	
ACORN (FENTON)								
Bowl, 7"-8½"	65	140	85	55	290	750	500AM	850
Plate, 9", Scarce		600		575				
ACORN (MILLERSBURG)								
Compote, Rare....................	3,000	1,800	1,900				2,850V	
ACORN BURRS (NORTHWOOD)								
Bowl, Flat, 10"	90	135	175				500	
Bowl, Flat, 5"	30	40	50				100	
Punch Bowl and Base	550	700	850	2,000		25,000	4,500W	
Punch Cup	45	90	100	75		575	100W	
Covered Butter	300	400	950				700	
Covered Sugar....................	225	300					450	
Creamer or Spooner	200	260					390	
Water Pitcher.....................	500	600	1,000					
Tumbler	65	80	100					
Whimsey Vase, Rare	3,000	3,500+						
ACORN AND FILE								
Ftd Compote, Rare..............							1,500V	
A DOZEN ROSES (IMPERIAL)								
Bowl, Footed, 8½"-10",								
Rare	650	750	850					
ADVERTISING ASHTRAY								
Various Designs..................	60+							
AFRICAN SHIELD (ENGLISH)								
Toothpick Holder (or								
Bud Holder)........................	115							
AGE HERALD (FENTON)								
Bowl, 9¼", Scarce		1,200						
Plate, 10", Scarce................		2,000						
AMARYLLIS (NORTHWOOD)								
Small Compote	225	200		275			450W	
Whimsey (Flattened)		600						
AMERICAN (FOSTORIA)								
Tumbler, Rare	95		125					
APOTHECARY JAR								
Small Size	60							
APPLE BLOSSOMS (DUGAN)								
Bowl, 7½"	40	58	70		175		150W	
Plate, 8¼"	250	275			260		300W	
APPLE BLOSSOM (ENAMELED) (NORTHWOOD)								
Tumbler				90				
APPLE BLOSSOM TWIGS (DUGAN)								
Bowl....................................	40	160	170			185	150W	
Plate...................................	200	250	300	190		400	225W	
APPLE PANELS (ENGLISH)								
Creamer	35							
Sugar (open)	35							
APPLE AND PEAR INTAGLIO (NORTHWOOD)								
Bowl, 10".............................	90							
Bowl, 5"...............................	40							
APPLE TREE (FENTON)								
Water Pitcher......................	225			500			750W	
Tumbler	40			65			150W	
Pitcher, Vase Whimsey,								
Rare	1,800			2,000				
APRIL SHOWERS (FENTON)								
Vase	55	110	150	130			200	
ARCADIA BASKETS								
Plate, 8"...............................	50							
ARCHED FLEUR-DE-LIS (HIGBEE)								
Mug, Rare	250							
ARCHED PANELS								
Tumbler	85							
ARCS (IMPERIAL)								
Bowls, 8½"...........................	40	60	50				175W	
Compote...............................	65	90						
ART DECO (ENGLISH)								
Bowl, 4"...............................	38							
ASTERS								
Bowl....................................	60							
Compote...............................	90							
ASTRAL								
Shade..................................	55							
AUGUST FLOWERS								
Shade..................................	42							
AURORA								
Bowl, 2 Sizes Decorated.......	400	700					950IM	
AUTUMN ACORNS (FENTON)								
Bowl, 8¼"	55	75	80	70				4,800
Plate, Rare..........................		1,000	1,000	1,200				

Aztec

Banded Rib

Basket

Beaded Acanthus

	M	A	G	B	PO	AO	Pas	R
AZTEC (McKEE)								
Pitcher, Rare	1,300							
Tumbler, Rare	650							
Creamer	250						250CM	
Sugar	250						250CM	
Rosebowl							400CM	
BABY BATHTUB (U.S. GLASS)								
Miniature Piece							500	
BABY'S BOUQUET								
Child's Plate, Scarce	115							
BAKER'S ROSETTE								
Ornament	75	90						
BALL AND SWIRL								
Mug	120							
BALLARD-MERCED, CA. (NORTHWOOD)								
Plate								
Bowl		950						
BALLOONS (IMPERIAL)								
Cake Plate	85						110SM	
Compote	65						90SM	
Perfume Atomizer	60						90SM	
Vase, 3 Sizes	75						100SM	
BAMBI								
Powder Jar w/lid	30							
BAMBOO BIRD								
Jar, Complete	800							
BAND (DUGAN)								
Violet Hat	30	40		75				
BANDED DIAMONDS & BARS								
Decanter, Complete	175							
Tumbler, Rare	425							
BANDED DIAMONDS & BARS (FINLAND)								
Tumbler, 4" tall	550							
Tumbler, 2¼" tall	550							
BANDED DIAMOND AND FAN (ENGLISH)								
Toothpick Holder	80							
BANDED DIAMONDS (CRYSTAL)								
Water Pitcher, Rare	900	1,250						
Tumbler, Rare	500	400						
Bowl, 10"	100	125						
Bowl, 5"	50	75						
BANDED GRAPE (FENTON)								
Water Pitcher	200		500	400			750W	
Tumbler	40		75	50			95W	
BANDED GRAPE AND LEAF (ENGLISH)								
Water Pitcher, Rare	650							
Tumbler, Rare	100							
BANDED KNIFE AND FORK								
One Shape	75							
BANDED PANELS (CRYSTAL)								
Open Sugar	45	60						
BANDED PORTLAND (U.S. GLASS)								
Puff Jar	80							
BANDED RIB								
Tumbler	25							
Pitcher	125							
BANDED ROSE								
Vase, Small	175							
BARBELLA (NORTHWOOD)								
Tumbler							225VAS	
BARBER BOTTLE (CAMBRIDGE)								
Complete	575	750	750					
BASKET (NORTHWOOD)								
Either Shape, Ftd	225	125	365	1,350		550	900CeB	
BASKETWEAVE (FENTON)								
Hat Shape-Advertising	50		65					
Vase Whimsey, Rare	750		900					450
Basket-Open Edge Jip	50	180	275	110			370IG	
Open Edge Plate, 10"	1,000			1,600			2,000IB	
Open Edge Bowl, 8"	140	175		190			290IG	
Open Edge Bowl, 5"	45	50	55	50			100W	
BASKETWEAVE AND CABLE (WESTMORELAND)								
Creamer, Complete	50	75	100				250W	
Sugar, Complete	50	75	100				250W	
Syrup Whimsey	180							
BEADED								
Hatpin		45						
BEADED ACANTHUS (IMPERIAL)								
Milk Pitcher	75		260				170SM	

5

Beaded Star

Beauty

Bernheimer

Big Basketweave

	M	A	G	B	PO	AO	Pas	R
BEADED BAND AND OCTAGON								
Kerosene Lamp	250							
BEADED BASKET (DUGAN)								
One shape	45	55	80	60			120V	
BEADED BERRY (FENTON)								
Exterior Pattern Only								
BEADED BULLSEYE (IMPERIAL)								
Vase, 8"-14"	47	125	140				130SM	
BEADED CABLE (NORTHWOOD)								
Rose Bowl	60	95	150	160	900	1,000	425W	
Candy Dish	50	70	80	85		500	200W	
BEADED HEARTS (NORTHWOOD)								
Bowl	50	85	90					
BEADED PANELS (IMPERIAL)								
Bowl, 8"	45							
Bowl, 5"	25							
Powder Jar w/lid	50							
BEADED PANELS (WESTMORELAND)								
Compote	45	55				115		
BEADED PANELS & GRAPES (CHECHOSLOVACIA)								
Tumbler	275							
BEADED SHELL (DUGAN)								
Bowl, Ftd, 9"	75	95						
Bowl, Ftd, 5"	35	40						
Mug	200	95						
Covered Butter	130	150						
Covered Sugar	90	110						
Creamer or Spooner	75	90						
Water Pitcher	500	650						
Tumbler	60	70		180				
Mug Whimsey		450						
BEADED SPEARS (CRYSTAL)								
Pitcher, Rare	490	560						
Tumbler, Rare	190	200						
BEADED STARS (FENTON)								
Plate, 9"	110							
Bowl	40				90			
Rose Bowl	60							
Banana Boat	110							
BEADED SWIRL (ENGLISH)								
Compote	50			60				
Covered Butter	70			85				
Milk Pitcher	75			90				
Sugar	50			55				
BEADS (NORTHWOOD)								
Bowl, 8½"	45	60	70					
BEADS AND BARS (U.S. GLASS)								
Spooner	55							
BEAUTY BUD VASE (DUGAN)								
Regular Size	40	85					80SM	
Twig Size, Rare	150	175						
BEAUTY BUD VASE VT.								
No Twigs	30						35SM	
BEETLE ASHTRAY (ARGENTINA)								
One Size, Rare				350				
BEETLE HATPIN								
Complete		85						
BELL FLOWER (DUGAN)								
Compote, handled				450				
BELLAIRE SOUVENIR (IMPERIAL)								
Bowl, Scarce	185							
BELLS AND BEADS (DUGAN)								
Bowl, 7½"	45	90	115	120				
Nappy	60	95			100			
Plate, 8"		170						
Hat Shape	40	60						
Compote	70	75						
Gravy Boat, Handled	55	70			140			
BERNHEIMER (MILLERSBURG)								
Bowl, 8¾", Scarce				1,900				
BERRY BASKET								
One Size	55							
Matching Shakers, Pair	75							
BIG BASKETWEAVE (DUGAN)								
Vase, 6"-14"	90	120			140	275	150W	
Basket, Small	45	60						
BIG CHIEF								
One Shape		95						
BIG FISH (MILLERSBURG)								
Bowl, Various Shapes	500	600	650				6,500V	
Banana Bowl, Rare		2,000	2,000					
Bowl, Tri-Cornered	1,050	2,000	2,000				2,000V	
Rose Bowl, Very Rare							7,500V	
Square Bowl, Very Rare	900	1,500	1,500				6,000V	

Black Bottom

Blackberry

Blackberry Wreath

Blocks and Arches

	M	A	G	B	PO	AO	Pas	R
BIG THISTLE (MILLERSBURG)								
Punch Bowl and Base Only, Rare		10,000						
BIRD OF PARADISE (NORTHWOOD)								
Bowl, Advertising		395						
Plate, Advertising		450						
BIRD WITH GRAPES (COCKATOO)								
Wall Vase	75							
BIRDS AND CHERRIES (FENTON)								
Bon-bon	45	65	65	65			90	
Bowl, 9½", Rare	200	325		375				
Bowl, 5", Rare	65	90						
Compote	45	60	65	60			95	
Plate, 10", Rare	1,200		1,600	1,500				
BLACK BOTTOM (FENTON)								
Candy Jar	60						60	
BLACKBERRY (FENTON)								
Open Edge Hat	40	45	50	40		175	80	475
Spittoon Whimsey, Rare	3,200			3,600				
Vase Whimsey, Rare	750			900			700W	
Plate, Rare	800			400				
BLACKBERRY (NORTHWOOD)								
Compote	55	65		75			100	
Bowl, Ftd, 9"	50	60						
BLACKBERRY BANDED (FENTON)								
Hat Shape	35		55	45	90			
BLACKBERRY BARK								
Vase, Rare		1,900*						
BLACKBERRY BLOCK (FENTON)								
Pitcher	265	1,250	1,500	600			6,500V	
Tumbler	50	150	85	75			300V	
BLACKBERRY BRAMBLE (FENTON)								
Bowl				60				
Compote	40	50	70	55				
BLACKBERRY, MINIATURE (FENTON)								
Compote, Small	125	250	350	265			590W	
Stemmed Plate, Rare				450				
BLACKBERRY SPRAY (FENTON)								
Bon-bon	35	45	50	45				
Compote	40	50	55	50				
Hat Shape	45	55	200	40		225	115V	485
BLACKBERRY WREATH (MILLERSBURG)								
Plate, 10", Rare	4,700	5,000						
Plate, 6", Rare	2,250	2,700	2,900					
Bowl, 5"	50	70	75				90CM	
Bowl, 7"-9"	65	90	90					
Bowl, 10", Ice Cream	175	200	250	1,100				
Spittoon Whimsey, Rare			3,800					
Plate, 8" Rare			4,200					
BLOCKS AND ARCHES								
Creamer	42							
BLOCKS AND ARCHES (CRYSTAL)								
Pitcher, Rare	100	140						
Tumbler, Rare	75	90						
BLOSSOMS AND BAND (IMPERIAL)								
Bowl, 10"	38	45						
Bowl, 5"	20	30						
Wall Vase, Complete	45							
BLOSSOM AND SPEARS								
Plate, 8"	52							
BLOSSOMTIME (NORTHWOOD)								
Compote	135	200	350					
BLOWN CANDLESTICKS								
One Size, Pair	90							
BLUEBERRY (FENTON)								
Pitcher, Scarce	500			700				
Tumbler, Scarce	60			100				
BO PEEP (WESTMORELAND)								
ABC Plate, Scarce	550							
Mug, Scarce	125							
BOOT								
One Shape	150							
BORDER PLANTS (DUGAN)								
Bowl, Flat, 8½"		125			180			
Bowl, Ftd, 8½"		600			250			
BOUQUET (FENTON)								
Pitcher	285			550			750W	
Tumbler	37	80		55			90W	

7

Boutonniere

Brocaded Acorns

Broacaded Palms

	M	A	G	B	PO	AO	Pas	R
BOUQUET AND LATTICE								
Various Shapes From $5.00-15.00 each, Late Carnival								
BOUQUET TOOTHPICK HOLDER								
One Size	75							
BOUTONNIERE (MILLERSBURG)								
Compote.............................	175	195	225					
BOW AND ENGLISH HOB (ENGLISH)								
Nut Bowl	50			60				
BOXED STAR								
One Shape, Rare							110	
BRIAR PATCH								
Hat Shape	40	50						
BRIDLE ROSETTE								
One Shape............................	85							
BROCADED ACORNS (FOSTORIA)								
BROCADED DAFFODILS								
BROCADED PALMS								
BROCADED ROSES								
BROCADED SUMMER GARDENS								
All Related Patterns in Similar Shapes and Colors								
Wine...................................							70	
Bon-bon							65	
Cake Tray...........................							110	
Ice Bucket							100	
Covered Box							95	
Tray							100	
Cake Plate, Center Handle ...							110	
Vase							120	
Rose Bowl............................							70	
Bowls, Various Sizes............							85	
Flower Set, 3 Pieces							190	
Center Bowl, Ftd.................							120	
BROKEN ARCHES (IMPERIAL)								
Bowl, 8½"-10"	45	50	75					
Punch Bowl and Base..........	365	595						
Punch Cup	30	30						
BROCKER'S (NORTHWOOD)								
Advertising Plate.................		1,700						
BROOKLYN								
Bottle w/stopper.................	75	95						
BROOKLYN BRIDGE (DUGAN)								
Bowl, Scarce.......................	350							
Unlettered Bowl, Rare..........	1,200							
BUBBLE BERRY								
Shade..................................							75	
BUBBLES								
Hatpin.................................		65						
Lamp Chimney							50	
BUDDHA (ENGLISH)								
One Shape, Rare	900						1,100IB	
BULL DOG								
Paperweight........................	350							
BULL'S EYE (U.S. GLASS)								
Oil Lamp	210							
BULL'S EYE AND LEAVES (NORTHWOOD)								
Bowl, 8½"	40	55	50					
BULL'S EYE AND LOOP (MILLERSBURG)								
Vase, 7"-11", Rare...............	300	400	500					
BULL'S EYE AND SPEARHEAD								
Wine...................................	90							
BUMBLEBEES								
Hatpin...............................		70						
BUNNY								
Bank	35							
BUTTERFLIES (FENTON)								
Bon-bon	60	70	75	65			90	
Card Tray	55			60				
BUTTERFLIES AND BELLS (CRYSTAL)								
Compote.............................	120	145						
BUTTERFLIES AND WARATAH (CRYSTAL)								
Compote, Large	120	200						
BUTTERFLY								
Pintray	40						50	

Butterfly

8

Butterfly and Berry

Butterfly and Tulip

Button and Daisy Hat

Cannon Ball Variant

	M	A	G	B	PO	AO	Pas	R
BUTTERFLY (FENTON)								
Ornament, Rare..................	190	220	225	200			300W	
BUTTERFLY (NORTHWOOD)								
Bon-bon, Regular	65	75	90	325				
Bon-bon, Ribbed Exterior		250					575IB	
BUTTERFLY (U.S. GLASS)								
Tumbler, Rare	5,800		6,000					
BUTTERFLY LAMP								
Oil Lamp	1,500							
BUTTERFLY AND BERRY (FENTON)								
Bowl, Ftd, 10"....................	100	200	250	225			750W	
Bowl, Ftd, 5"......................	35	40	45	40			95W	1,200
Covered Butter	150	240	300	225				
Covered Sugar	100	160	200	175				
Covered Creamer	100	150	200	170				
Nut Bowl Whimsey		700						
Spooner.............................	90	125	190	160				
Pitcher..............................	350	500		490			1,200W	
Tumbler	40	70	80	70			100W	
Hatpin Holder, Rare............	790			650				
Vase, Rare	40	55	200	50			500W	700
Spittoon Whimsey, 2 Types..		2,600		2,600				
Bowl Whimsey (Fernery)	850	1,200		1,400				
Plate, Ftd (Whimsey)............				1,500				
BUTTERFLY BOWER (CRYSTAL)								
Compote.............................	95	130						
Cake Plate, Stemmed..........		200						
BUTTERFLY BUSH (CRYSTAL)								
Compote, Large	120	175						
BUTTERFLY AND CORN (NORTHWOOD)								
Vase, Rare							4,000V	
BUTTERFLY AND FERN (FENTON)								
Pitcher..............................	450	575	650	960				
Tumbler	55	60	85	65				
BUTTERFLY AND TULIP (DUGAN)								
Bowl, Ftd, 10½", Scarce	490	2,500						
Bowl, Whimsey Shape, Rare ..	900	1,500						
BUTTERMILK, PLAIN (FENTON)								
Goblet	60	70	80					
BUTTON AND FAN								
Hatpin................................		60						
BUTTONS AND DAISY (IMPERIAL)								
Hat (Old Only)							70CM	
Slipper (Old Only)							80CM	
BUTTRESS (U.S. GLASS)								
Pitcher, Rare......................	400							
Tumbler, Rare	300							
BUZZ SAW								
Shade................................	45							
BUZZ SAW (CAMBRIDGE)								
Cruet, Small 4", Rare..........			400					
Cruet, Large 6", Rare	400		400					
CACTUS (MILLERSBURG)								
Exterior Pattern								
CANADA DRY								
Bottle................................	55							
CANDLE LAMP (FOSTORIA)								
One Size	110						150AM	
CANE (IMPERIAL)								
Bowl, 7½"-10"......................	40						50	
Pickle Dish	32						46	
Wine	65						75	
Compote.............................	80						115	
CANE AND DAISY CUT (JENKINS)								
Vase	150							
Basket, Handled, Rare.........	220						250	
CANE AND SCROLL (SEA THISTLE) (ENGLISH)								
Rose Bowl	55			75				
Creamer or Sugar	45							
CANNONBALL VT.								
Pitcher..............................	240			285			400W	
Tumbler	50			65			90W	
CANOE (U.S. GLASS)								
One Size	150							
CAPITOL (WESTMORELAND)								
Mug, Small	140							
Bowl, Ftd, Small		70		70				

Captive Rose

Cartwheel

Checkerboard

Cherry (Dugan)

	M	A	G	B	PO	AO	Pas	R
CAPTIVE ROSE (FENTON)								
Bowl, 8½"-10"	75	90	90	80			250BA	
Compote	65	80	90	160				
Plate, 7"	140	190	210	200			550	
Plate, 9"	225	410	425	400				
Bon-bon	50		70	60			160	
CARNATION (NEW MARTINSVILLE)								
Punch Cup	57							
CARNIVAL BELL								
One Size	425							
CARNIVAL HONEYCOMB (IMPERIAL)								
Bon-bon	40	55	60				75AM	
Creamer or Sugar	35							
Plate, 7"		95						
Bowl, Handles, 6"	30							
CAROLINA DOGWOOD (WESTMORELAND)								
Bowl, 8½"	80	110			260MO	500		
Plate, Rare					320MO			
CAROLINE (DUGAN)								
Bowl, 7"-10"	70				190			
Banana Bowl					210			
Basket, Scarce					400			
CARRIE (ANCHOR-HOCKING)								
One Size	60							
CARTWHEEL #411 (HEISEY)								
Compote	50							
Goblet	75							
CATHEDRAL (SWEDEN) (Also know as Curved Star)								
Chalice, 7"	145		190					
Pitcher, Rare			3,700					
Bowl, 10"	50							
Flower Holder	75							
Epergne, Scarce	245							
Compote, 2 Sizes	60		80					
Creamer, Ftd	60							
Butterdish, 2 Sizes	240							
CATHEDRAL ARCHES (ENGLISH)								
Punch Bowl, 1 Piece	350							
CATTAILS								
Hatpin		50						
CENTRAL SHOE STORE (NORTHWOOD)								
Bowl, 6"-7"		1,200						
CHAIN AND STAR (FOSTORIA)								
Tumbler, Rare	900							
Covered Butter, Rare	1,500							
CHATELAINE (IMPERIAL)								
Pitcher, Rare		3,700						
Tumbler, Rare		510						
CHATHAM (U.S. GLASS)								
Compote	75							
Candlesticks, Pair	90							
CHECKERBOARD BOUQUET								
Plate, 8"		85						
CHECKERBOARD (WESTMORELAND)								
Cruet, Rare							750CL	
Pitcher, Rare		3,800						
Tumbler, Rare	750	550						
Goblet, Rare	350	425						
Punch Cup	90							
Wine, Rare	295							
Vase		2,700						
CHECKERBOARD PANELS (ENGLISH)								
Bowl	70							
CHECKERS								
Ashtray	47							
Bowl, 4"	28							
Bowl, 9"	40							
Butter, 2 Sizes	200							
Plate, 7"	90							
CHERRY (DUGAN)								
Bowl, Flat, 5"	40	50			90			
Bowl, Flat, 8"	65	70			210			
Bowl, Ftd, 8½"	210	310			400			
Plate, 6"		200			410			
Cruet, Rare							650W	
CHERRY (FENTON) (See Mikado Compote)								

Cherry Chain

Cherry Circle

Circle Scroll

Classic Arts

	M	A	G	B	PO	AO	Pas	R
CHERRY								
(MILLERSBURG)								
Bowl, 4"	60	85	90	600				
Bowl, 5", Hobnail								
Exterior Rare				900				
Bowl, 7", Rare	135	95	130					
Bowl, 9", Scarce	90	125	150					
Bowl, Ice Cream, 10"	250	375	350	1,800				
Bowl, 9", Hobnail								
Exterior Rare	900	1,250		2,700				
Compote, Large, Rare	1,250	1,495	1,600	4,000			5,000V	
Banana Compote, Rare		4,000						
Milk Pitcher, Rare	1,100							
Plate, 6", Rare	1,050							
Plate, 7½", Rare		1,100	1,150					
Plate, 10", Rare	4,600							
Powder Jar, Rare			1,950					
Covered Butter	250	375	450					
Covered Sugar	170	300	325					
Creamer or Spooner	150	275	275					
Pitcher, Scarce	1,150	1,000	1,450					
Tumbler, 2 Variations	145	190	210					
CHERRY BLOSSOMS								
Pitcher				150				
Tumbler				40				
CHERRY AND CABLE								
(NORTHWOOD)								
Pitcher, Rare	1,450							
Tumbler, Rare	425							
Bowl, 5", Scarce	75							
Butter, Rare	450							
Sugar, Creamer,								
Spooner, Each, Rare	210							
Bowl, 9", Scarce	125							
CHERRY AND CABLE INTAGLIO								
(NORTHWOOD)								
Bowl, 10"	75							
Bowl, 5"	50							
CHERRY CHAIN (FENTON)								
Bon-bon	50	60	65	55				
Bowl, 6½"-10"	50	90	90	95				
Plate, 7"-9"	85			140				
CHERRY CIRCLES								
(FENTON)								
Bon-bon	50	65		75				7,400
Bowl, 8"	50	65		70				
Compote	70	80		80			130W	
Plate, 9", Rare	550			210			210W	
CHERRY AND DAISIES								
(FENTON)								
Banana Boat	950			1,050				
CHERRY SMASH								
(U.S. GLASS)								
Bowl, 8"	65							
Butter	150							
Tumbler	190							
CHERRY STIPPLED								
Tumbler	110							
CHERUB								
Lamp, Rare							150	
CHIPPENDALE SOUVENIR								
Creamer or Sugar	65	80						
CHRISTMAS COMPOTE								
Large Compote, Rare	4,200	4,700						
CHRYSANTHEMUM								
(FENTON)								
Bowl, Flat, 9"	130	60	95	80				5,700
Bowl, Ftd, 10"	80	75	110	120			600BA	
CHRYSANTHEMUM DRAPE								
Oil Lamp, Rare							900	
CIRCLE SCROLL (DUGAN)								
Compote, Scarce		150						
Bowl, 10"	65	80						
Bowl, 5"	40	45						
Pitcher, Rare	2,000	2,800						
Tumbler, Rare	400	600						
Hat Shape, Rare	60	100						
Creamer or Spooner	150	225						
Vase Whimsey, Rare	135	160						
Butter or Sugar	375	425						
CLASSIC ARTS (CZECH)								
Vase, 7" (Egyptian)	700							
Powder Jar	575							
Rose Bowl	525							
Vase, 10", Rare	750							
CLEOPATRA								
Bottle	110							

11

Cleveland Memorial

Cobblestone

Colonial

Concord

	M	A	G	B	PO	AO	Pas	R
CLEVELAND MEMORIAL (MILLERSBURG)								
Ashtray, Rare	5,800	5,700						
COAL BUCKET (U.S. GLASS)								
One Size	400		500					
COBBLESTONES (DUGAN)								
Bowl, 9"	65	150						
Bowl, 5"	40	80						
COBBLESTONES (DUGAN-IMPERIAL)								
Plate, Rare		1,300						
COBBLESTONES (IMPERIAL)								
Bowl, 5"	35	40	50					
Bowl, 8½"	75	275	115					
Bon-bon	45	75	70				95AM	
COIN DOT (FENTON)								
Bowl, 6"-10"	35	40	40	65		260	100LV	1,200
Plate, 9", Rare	200	250	275	260				
Pitcher, Rare	350	500	550	525				
Tumbler, Rare	190	250	265	225				
Basket Whimsey, Rare	75			100				
Rose Bowl	90							1,600
COIN DOT VT. (WESTMORELAND)								
Compote	60				175MO	270	350IBO	
Rose Bowl	40	75					320TL	
Bowl	40	60	70				90	
COIN SPOT (DUGAN)								
Compote	45	60	70	65	200	375		
Goblet, Rare							390IG	
COLOGNE BOTTLE (CAMBRIDGE)								
One Size, Rare	600		850					
COLONIAL (IMPERIAL)								
Lemonade Goblet	75							
Vase	40	60						
Toothpick Holder	60	110	95					
Open Sugar or Creamer	47							
Candlesticks, Pair	200							
COLONIAL LADY (IMPERIAL)								
Vase, Rare	1,000	1,150						
COLUMBIA (IMPERIAL)								
Vase	45	55	50					
Compote	60	75	65					
COLUMBUS								
Plate, 8"	45							
COMPASS (DUGAN) (Exterior Pattern Only)								
COMPOTE VASE								
Stemmed Shape	50	65	72	76				
CONCAVE DIAMONDS (DUGAN)								
Pitcher w/lid			450RG				550V	
Tumbler			425RG				190V	
Pickle Castor, Ornate Holder	475						395CeB	
Tumble-Up, Complete, Rare							230V	
Coaster, Not Iridized							20	
Vase							100CeB	
CONCAVE FLUTE (WESTMORELAND)								
Rose Bowl	50		65					
Vase	40	65	65					
CONCORD (FENTON)								
Bowl, 9", Scarce	175	300	400	250			350AM	
Plate, 10", Rare	800	1,200	1,300				1,000AM	
CONE AND TIE (IMPERIAL)								
Tumbler, Rare		950						
CONNIE (NORTHWOOD)								
Pitcher							750W	
Tumbler							125W	
CONSTELLATION (DUGAN)								
Compote	150	60			200		175V	
CONTINENTAL BOTTLE								
2 Sizes	45							
COOLEEMEE, NC (FENTON)								
Advertising Plate, Rare (Heart and Vine)	1,500							
CORAL (FENTON)								
Bowl, 9"	200		395	400			500W	
Compote	450		500				650W	
Plate, 9½", Rare	1,000		1,200	1,200				
CORINTH (DUGAN)								
Bowl, 9"	40	50			200			
Banana Dish	55	75			300			
CORINTH (WESTMORELAND)								
Vase	30	50	75	450BO	150		60TL	
Bowl	40	60					75TL	
CORN BOTTLE (IMPERIAL)								
One Size	285		250				275SM	

Corn Cruet

Corn Vase

Coronation

Covered Swan

	M	A	G	B	PO	AO	Pas	R
CORN CRUET								
One Size, Rare							1,100W	
CORN VASE (NORTHWOOD)								
Regular Mold	1,150	800	900	2,200		4,800	2,500TL	
Pulled Husk, Rare		7,500	7,500					
Fancy Husk, Rare (Dugan)	950							
CORNING (CORNING)								
Insulator	35+							
CORNUCOPIA (FENTON)								
Candlestick, pair, 5"	80						190W	
Vase, 5"	70						110W	
Candle Holder, 6½"							110W	
CORONATION (ENGLISH)								
Vase, 5" (Victoria Crown Design)	250							
COSMOS (MILLERSBURG)								
Bowl, 5"			70					
COSMOS AND CANE								
Bowl, 10"	75						90W	
Bowl, 5"	40						45W	
Compote, Tall, Rare	350						300W	
Butter, Covered	200						300W	
Covered Sugar or Creamer	135						200W	
Flat Tray, Rare							275W	
Spooner	100						195W	
Stemmed Dessert							150W	
Pitcher, Rare	750						1,450W	
Tumbler, Rare	115						250W	
Advertising Tumbler, Rare							110AM	
Rose Bowl, Large	1,275	1,500					2,000AM	
Rose Bowl Whimsey	1,700							
Spittoon Whimsey, Rare							4,200W	
Chop Plate, Rare	1,450						1,600W	
Breakfast Set, 2 Pieces							500W	
COSMOS & HOBSTAR								
Bowl (on metal stand)	450							
COSMOS VT. (FENTON)								
Bowl, 9"-10"	40	65		75			75V	485
Plate, 10", Rare	175	210			400			
COUNTRY KITCHEN (MILLERSBURG)								
Bowl, 9", Rare	265							
Bowl, 5", Rare	90							
Spittoon Whimsey, Rare		4,600						
Covered Butter, Rare	650	750						
Sugar, Creamer or Spooner	400	500	800				900V	
Vase Whimsey, Rare	600	700						
COURTHOUSE (MILLERSBURG								
Lettered (Round or Ruffled), Scarce		950						
Unlettered, Rare		2,500						
COVERED FROG (HEISEY)								
One Size	375	450	500	275			650	
COVERED HEN (ENGLISH)								
One Size	110			145				
COVERED LITTLE HEN (TINY)								
Miniature, 3½", Rare							90CM	
COVERED MALLARD (U.S. GLASS)								
One Shape							450CM	
COVERED SWAN (ENGLISH)								
One Size	150	250						
COVERED TURKEY (HEISEY)								
One Size		400						
COVERED TURTLE (HEISEY)								
One Size			475				600PK	
CR (ARGENTINA)								
Ash Tray	90			135				
CRAB CLAW (IMPERIAL)								
Bowl, 5"	25	37	40					
Bowl, 10"	50	65	65				70SM	
Fruit Bowl w/base	110							
Pitcher, Scarce	650							
Tumbler, Scarce	140							
Cruet, Rare	950							

Crucifix

Cut Flowers

Daisy

Daisy and Cane

	M	A	G	B	PO	AO	Pas	R
CRACKLE (IMPERIAL)								
Auto Vase	30	35	35					
Bowl, 9"	25	30	30					
Bowl, 5"	15	18	18					
Candy Jar w/lid	30							
Candlestick, 3½"	25							
Candlestick, 7"	30							
Plate	45	55	60					
Punch Bowl and Base	55							
Punch Cup	10							
Pitcher, Dome Base	90	150	160					
Spittoon, Large	45							
Tumbler, Dome Base	20	30	30					
Wall Vase	40							
Window Planter, Rare	110							
CROCUS VT.								
Tumbler	45	65						
CRUCIFIX (IMPERIAL)								
Candlestick, Rare, Each	650							
CRYSTAL CUT (CRYSTAL)								
Compote	75							
CUBA (McKee)								
Goblet, Rare	45							
CURTAIN OPTIC (FENTON)								
Pitcher							450VAS	
Tumbler							150VAS	
Guest Set (tumble-up)							350VAS	
CUT ARCHES (ENGLISH)								
Banana Bowl	80							
CUT ARCS (FENTON)								
Bowl, 7½"-10"	40							
Compote	55	60		55				
Vase Whimsey (From Bowl)	40	50		50			80W	
CUT COSMOS (MILLERSBURG)								
Tumbler, Rare	450							
CUT CRYSTAL (U.S. GLASS)								
Compote, 5½"	110							
Water Bottle	185							
CUT FLOWERS (JENKINS)								
Vase, 10"	200							
CUT OVALS (FENTON)								
Candlesticks, pair	175						210	700
Bowl, 7"-10"	60						75	425
CUT SPRAYS								
Vase, 9"	45			75				
DAHLIA (DUGAN)								
Bowl, Ftd, 10"	95	125					290W	
Bowl, Ftd, 5"	40	50					190W	
Butter	120	155					350W	
Sugar	90	100					250W	
Creamer or Spooner	75	90					220W	
Pitcher, Rare	500	950					800W	
Tumbler, Rare	90	145					170W	
DAHLIA (FENTON)								
Twist Epergne, One Lily	250						300W	
DAHLIA AND DRAPE (FENTON)								
Tumble-Up, Complete	150						190IB	
DAINTY BUD VASE								
One Size	55							
DAISY (FENTON)								
Bon-bon, Scarce	250			300				
DAISY BASKET (IMPERIAL)								
One Size	65						85SM	
DAISY BLOCK (ENGLISH)								
Rowboat, Scarce	250	300					300AQ	
DAISY AND CANE (ENGLISH)								
Vase	75							
Decanter, Rare	90							
Spittoon, Rare				250				
DAISY CHAIN								
Shade	50							
DAISY CUT BELL (FENTON)								
One Size, Rare	500							

Daisy and Plume

Diamond and Daisy Cut

Diamond Flutes

	M	A	G	B	PO	AO	Pas	R
DAISY AND DRAPE (NORTHWOOD)								
Vase	300	375	2,200	550		700	400W	
DAISY DEAR (DUGAN)								
Bowl	40	48			55		70W	
DAISY IN OVAL PANELS (U.S. GLASS)								
Creamer or Sugar, Each	55							
DAISY AND PLUME (NORTHWOOD)								
Rose Bowl, 2 Shapes	75	100	105	110	175	2,000	550	
Compote	60	110	90	100	160			
Candy Dish	70	90	90	100	165			
DAISY SQUARES								
Rose Bowl	600		675				650IG	
Goblet, Rare	700	900					800AM	
Compote, Rare	500						700AM	
DAISY WEB (DUGAN)								
Hat, Rare	180	500			650			
DAISY WREATH (WESTMORELAND)								
Bowl, 8"-10"		250				600	500MO	
DANCE OF THE VEILS (FENTON)								
Vase, Rare	3,000							
DANDELION (NORTHWOOD)								
Mug	500	575	675	500		650	750BO	
Pitcher	395	620	700	900			7,500IB	
Tumbler	175	190	200	250			475IG	
Vase Whimsey, Rare		850						
DAVISON'S SOCIETY CHOCOLATES (NORTHWOOD)								
Plate, Handgrip		700						
DECO LILY								
Bulbous Vase	140							
DEEP GRAPE (MILLERSBURG)								
Compote, Rare	1,200	1,500	1,700	3,000				
Compote, Ruffled Top, Rare		2,400						
Rose Bowl, Stemmed			8,000					
DeVILBISS								
Atomizer, Complete	65+							
Perfumer	60+							
DIAMONDS (MILLERSBURG)								
Pitcher	285	395	350				490AQ	
Tumbler	70	100	85				190AQ	
Punch Bowl and Base, Rare	2,800	2,300	2,500					
Pitcher Oddity (No Spout)		550	550					
Spittoon Whimsey, Very Rare	8000*							
DIAMOND BAND (CRYSTAL)								
Open Sugar	45	60						
Float Set	400	550						
DIAMOND BAND AND FAN (ENGLISH)								
Cordial Set, Complete, Rare	900							
DIAMOND CHECKERBOARD								
Cracker Jar	85							
Butter	90							
Bowl, 9"	40							
Bowl, 5"	25							
Tumbler	100							
DIAMOND DAISY								
Plate, 8"	95							
DIAMOND AND DAISY CUT (U.S. GLASS)								
Vase, Square, 10"	125							
Compote	55	70		75				
Pitcher, Rare	400			450				
Tumbler, Rare	50			60				
DIAMOND AND DAISY CUT VT (JENKINS)								
Punch Bowl/Base, Rare	600							
DIAMOND AND FILE								
Banana Bowl	65							
Bowl, 7"-9"	50						70	
DIAMOND FLUTES (U.S. GLASS)								
Creamer	45							
Parfait	55							

Diamond Ovals

Diamond Pinwheel

Diamond Point

	M	A	G	B	PO	AO	Pas	R
DIAMOND FOUNTAIN (HIGBEE)								
Cruet, Rare......................	750*							
DIAMOND LACE (IMPERIAL)								
Bowl, 10"-11"	65	110						
Bowl, 5".............................	30	40						
Pitcher...............................		295						
Tumbler	190	70					250W*	
DIAMOND OVALS (ENGLISH)								
Compote (Open Sugar).........	40							
Creamer	40							
DIAMOND PINWHEEL (ENGLISH)								
Compote............................	45							
Butter	75							
DIAMOND POINT								
Rose Bowl..........................	700							
Basket, Rare......................	1,350	1,400		1,500				
DIAMOND POINT COLUMNS (IMPERIAL)								
Bowl, 4½"	20							
Compote............................	30						40	
Plate, 7"............................	35							
Vase	40	55					55	
Butter	70							
Creamer, Sugar or Spooner, Each	40							
Powder Jar w/lid	40							
Milk Pitcher.......................	35							
DIAMOND POINTS (NORTHWOOD)								
Vase, 7"-14".......................	45	90	80	175	300	395	275TL	
DIAMOND PRISMS (ENGLISH)								
Compote.............................	58							
DIAMOND AND RIB (FENTON)								
Vase, 7"-12".......................	45	100	90	80			70SM	
Funeral Vase, 17"-22"	700	900	1,000	1,000			800W	
Vase Whimsey			900					
DIAMOND RING (IMPERIAL)								
Rose Bowl, Rare	400*	650*					450*SM	
Bowl, 9".............................	40	50					55SM	
Bowl, 5".............................	25	30					32SM	
Fruit Bowl, 9½"..................	65	90					60SM	
DIAMOND STAR								
Mug, 2 sizes	120+							
Vase, 8"	80							
DIAMOND AND SUNBURST (IMPERIAL)								
Bowl, 8".............................	50	55	55				50AM	
Decanter	110	150	150					
Wine..................................	55	60	60					
Oil Cruet, Rare		900*						
DIAMOND TOP (ENGLISH)								
Creamer	40							
Spooner..............................	40							
DIAMOND VANE (ENGLISH)								
Creamer, 4"	35							
DIVING DOLPHINS (ENGLISH)								
Bowl, Ftd, 7"......................	200	260	280	270				
DOG								
Ashtray	85							
DOGWOOD SPRAYS (DUGAN)								
Compote.............................	270				360			
Bowl, 9"..............................	250	270			370			
DOLPHINS (MILLERSBURG)								
Compote, Rare.....................		1,850	2,000	6,000				
DORSEY AND FUNKENSTEIN (NORTHWOOD)								
Plate..................................		600						
DOTS AND CURVES								
Hatpin................................		55						
DOTTED DAISIES								
Plate, 8"..............................	90							
DOTTED DIAMONDS & DAISIES								
Tumbler	90							

Double Dutch

Double Scroll

Double Stem Rose

Dragon's Tongue

	M	A	G	B	PO	AO	Pas	R
DOUBLE DOLPHINS (FENTON)								
Bowl, Ftd, 9"-11"							115	
Cake Plate, Center Handle							85	
Candlesticks, pair							90	
Compote							70	
Fan Vapse							70	
Covered Candy Dish, Stemmed							80	
Bowl, 8"-10", Flat							65	
DOUBLE DUTCH (IMPERIAL)								
Bowl, 9", Ftd	50	75	75				85SM	
DOUBLE LOOP (NORTHWOOD)								
Creamer	155	160	170	190		275		
Sugar	155	160	170	190		290		
DOUBLE SCROLL (IMPERIAL)								
Bowl	45	55	55				65	210
Candlesticks, pair	75	80	80				80	260
Punch Cup	25							
DOUBLE STAR (CAMBRIDGE)								
Pitcher, Scarce	750	650	500					
Tumbler, Scarce	280	140	60					
Spittoon Whimsey, Rare		3,000						
Bowl, 9", Rare			400					
DOUBLE STEM ROSE (DUGAN)								
Bowl, Dome Base, 8½"	100	90	115	100	190		600CeB	
DOUGHNUT BRIDLE ROSETTE								
One Size		95						
DRAGON AND LOTUS (FENTON)								
Bowl, Flat, 9"	185	150	195	115	240	2,400	875AM	4,800
Bowl, Ftd, 9"	180	195	175	190	200		85LV	4,500
Plate, 9½", Rare	2,800	1,350		1,600	1,100		1200	9,000
DRAGON AND STRAWBERRY (FENTON)								
Bowl, Flat, 9", Scarce	450		900	950		2,300		
Bowl, Ftd, 9", Scarce	400		900	795				
Plate (Absentee Dragon), Rare	3,700							
DRAGON VASE								
Square Vase		250						
DRAGONFLY								
Shade							65	
DRAGONFLY LAMP								
Oil Lamp, Rare							1,800	
DRAGON'S TONGUE (FENTON)								
Bowl, 11", Scarce	950							
Shade	40				115			
DRAPE AND TASSEL								
Shade	45							
DRAPERY (NORTHWOOD)								
Vase	45	235	110	225EB		250	250IG	
Rose Bowl	240	135	170	120		700	600W	
Candy Dish	65	140	200	110		550	200AQ	
DRAPERY VT. (FENTON)								
Pitcher, Rare	510							
Tumbler, Scarce	90							
DREIBUS PARFAIT SWEETS (NORTHWOOD)								
Plate, Handgrip, 6"		550						
DUCKIE								
Powder Jar w/lid	40							
DUGAN FAN (DUGAN)								
Sauce, 5"	40	55			145			
Gravy Boat, Ftd	65	75			210		100	
DUGAN'S MANY RIBS								
Vase	60	80		75	110			
Hat Shape	50	70		60	100			
DUNCAN (NATIONAL GLASS)								
Cruet	600							
DURAND (FENTON)								
Bowl - Grape and Cable					1,200			
DUTCH MILL								
Plate, 8"	50							
Ashtray	65							

Elks (Millersburg)

Embroidered Mums

Engraved Grape

Estate

	M	A	G	B	PO	AO	Pas	R
DUTCH PLATE								
One Size, 8"..........................	55							
DUTCH TWINS								
Ashtray	50							
E.A. HUDSON FURNITURE (NORTHWOOD)								
Plate..................................		1,000						
EAGLE FURNITURE (NORTHWOOD)								
Plate..................................		800						
EAT PARADISE SODA (NORTHWOOD)								
....		595						
EBON								
Vase		110BA						
ELEGANCE								
Bowl, 8¼", Rare	2,800						3,200IB	
Plate, Rare...........................							4,800IB	
ELKS (DUGAN)								
Nappy, Very Rare.................		4,200						
ELKS (FENTON)								
Detroit Bowl, Scarce	1,300	900	750	700				
Parkersburg Plate, Rare			1,450	1,300				
Atlantic City Plate, Rare			1,800	1,200				
Atlantic City Bowl...............				1,325				
1911 Atlantic City Bell, Rare				2,200				
1917 Portland Bell, Rare				15,000*				
1914 Parkersburg Bell, Rare				2,300				
ELKS (MILLERSBURG)								
Bowl, Rare.......................		1,500						
Paperweight, Rare...............		1,500	1,700					
EMBROIDERED MUMS (NORTHWOOD)								
Bowl, 9".............................	475	400	585	450		3,900	1,950IG	
Stemmed Bon-bon..............							1,250W	
Plate..................................	600	550	695	650			2,500IG	
EMU (CRYSTAL)								
Bowl, 5", Rare.....................	75							
Bowl, 10", Rare...................	245						550AM	
ENAMELLED GRAPE (NORTHWOOD)								
Pitcher..............................				400				
Tumbler				45				
ENAMELED PANEL								
Goblet	190							
ENGLISH BUTTON BAND (ENGLISH)								
Creamer	45							
Sugar	45							
ENGLISH HOB AND BUTTON (ENGLISH)								
Bowl, 7"-10"	60	80	95	70				
Epergne (metal base), Rare	125			145				
ENGRAVED DAISY & SPEARS								
Goblet, 4½".........................	75							
ENGRAVED FLORAL (FENTON)								
Tumbler			95					
ENGRAVED GRAPES (FENTON)								
Vase, 8"	65						75	
Candy Jar w/lid	85							
Juice Glass.........................	30							
Pitcher, Squat.....................	120							
Tumbler	30							
Pitcher, Tall	145							
Tumble-Up	150							
ESTATE (WESTMORELAND)								
Mug, Rare	75							
Perfume..............................							1,100SM	
Creamer or Sugar	55				90	190BO	110AQ	
Bud Vase, 6".......................	50						65	
ESTATE, STIPPLED (WESTMORELAND)								
Vase, 3"					190		200	

Evelyn

Fan-Tail

Fan

Farmyard

	M	A	G	B	PO	AO	Pas	R
ETCHED DECO								
Plate, ftd. 8".............	60							
EVELYN (FOSTORIA)								
Bowl (1940's)......................			1,000*					
EXCHANGE BANK (NORTHWOOD)								
Plate, 6"......................		500						
EYE CUP								
One Size...........................	90							
FAMOUS								
Puff box..........................	75							
FANCIFUL (DUGAN)								
Bowl, 8½".........................	90	350		500EB		250	175W	
Plate, 9".........................	175	550		350		500	250W	
FANCY (NORTHWOOD)								
(Interior on some "Fine Cut and Roses" Rose Bowls)								
FANCY CUT (ENGLISH)								
Miniature Pitcher, Rare........	225							
Miniature Tumbler	60							
FANCY FLOWERS (IMPERIAL)								
Compote............................	120		175					
FANS (ENGLISH)								
Pitcher............................	185							
Cracker Jar (metal lid).........	150							
Tumbler	150							
FANTAIL (FENTON)								
Bowl, Ftd, 5".....................	80			220			145	
Bowl, Ftd, 9".....................	110			275			180	
Compote...........................	90			195				
Plate, Ftd, Rare..................				1,600				
FARMYARD (DUGAN)								
Bowl, 10", Rare..................		3,200	8,500		10,000			
Plate, 10½", Very Rare.........		12,000						
FASHION (IMPERIAL)								
Creamer or Sugar	42	125					50	
Fruit Bowl and Base	70						75	
Punch Bowl and Base.........	85	195					90	
Punch Cup	24	40					30	
Pitcher............................	250	1,000					600SM	
Tumbler	20	225					100SM	
Bowl, 9"...........................	40		90				55SM	
Bride's Basket	125						140	
Butter	75	200						
Rose Bowl, Rare	450	1,300	950					
FEATHER AND HEART (MILLERSBURG)								
Pitcher, Scarce....................	600	750	850					
Tumbler, Scarce	75	150	200					
FEATHER STITCH (FENTON)								
Bowl, 8½"-10".....................	60	80	90	80				
FEATHER SWIRL (U.S. GLASS)								
Vase	65							
Butter	165							
FEATHERED ARROW (ENGLISH)								
Bowl, 8½"	50							
FEATHERED SERPENT (FENTON)								
Bowl, 5".............................	30	40	45	42				
Bowl, 10"...........................	60	75	70	65				
Spittoon Whimsey, Rare		4,000						
FEATHERS (NORTHWOOD)								
Vase, 7"-12".......................	60	85	95	105				
FELDMAN BROTHERS (NORTHWOOD)								
Bowl..................................		550						
FENTONIA								
Bowl, Ftd, 9½"	60	85	75	70				
Bowl, Ftd, 5"	30	50	40	40				
Fruitbowl, 10"....................	85			90				
Butter	115			185				
Creamer, Sugar or Spooner..........................	75			85				
Pitcher..............................	390			600				
Tumbler	50			75				
FENTONIA FRUIT (FENTON)								
Bowl, Ftd, 6"......................	45			55				
Bowl, Ftd, 10".....................	120			160				
Pitcher, Rare......................	575			700				
Vase Whimsey, Rare	140			160				
Tumbler, Rare	150			200				
FENTON'S ARCHED FLUTE (FENTON)								
Toothpick Holder	85			100			140	

19

	M	A	G	B	PO	AO	Pas	R
FENTON'S BASKET (FENTON)								
Two Row or Three Row (Open Edge)	45		225	150			325CeB	460
Advertising	65							
FERN (FENTON)								
Bowl, 7"-9", Rare				900*				
FERN (NORTHWOOD)								
Bowl, 6½"-9"	50	65	70					
Compote	55	70	85	100			110	
Hat, Rare	90	120	135				160	
FERN BRAND CHOCOLATES (NORTHWOOD)								
Plate		800						
FERN PANELS (FENTON)								
Hat	45		60	50			495	
FIELD FLOWER (IMPERIAL)								
Pitcher, Scarce	165	350	365	400			360AM	
Tumbler, Scarce	35	60	70	150			90AM	1,500
Milk Pitcher, Rare	180	200	220				225AM	
FIELD THISTLE (U.S. GLASS)								
Plate, 6", Rare	180							
Plate, 9" Rare	350							
Butter, Rare	125							
Sugar, Creamer or Spooner, Rare	80							
Compote, Large	90							
Pitcher, Scarce	160							
Tumbler, Scarce	45							
Breakfast Set, 2 Pc, Rare							350IB	
Bowl, 6"-10"	45						290LG	
Vase	65							
FILE (IMPERIAL AND ENGLISH)								
Pitcher, Rare	265	445						
Tumbler, Scarce	150							
Bowl, 5"	30	40						
Bowl, 7"-10"	45+	50					60	
Compote	40	50					60	
Vase	75							
Butter	190							
Creamer or Spooner	100							
Sugar	120							
FILE AND FAN								
Bowl, Ftd, 6"	40				160			
Compote						290	125MO	
FINE BLOCK (IMPERIAL)								
Shade			45					
FINE CUT FLOWERS AND VT. (FENTON)								
Compote	50		75					
Goblet	50		75					
FINE CUT HEART (MILLERSBURG)								
(Primrose Bowl Exterior Pattern)								
FINE CUT OVALS (MILLERSBURG)								
(Whirling Leaves Exterior Pattern)								
FINE CUT RINGS (ENGLISH)								
Oval Bowl	40							
Vase	50							
Celery	60							
Butter	70							
Creamer	45							
Stemmed Sugar	45							
Stemmed Cake Stand	75							
Round Bowl	35							
Jam Jar w/lid	65							
FINE CUT AND ROSES (NORTHWOOD)								
Rose Bowl, Ftd	100	115	200	220		1,000	1,000IG	
Candy Dish, Ftd	85	90	170	185		900	260W	
(Add 25% for Fancy Interior)								
FINE PRISMS AND DIAMONDS (ENGLISH)								
Vase, 7"-14"							90AM	
FINE RIB (NORTHWOOD, FENTON AND DUGAN)								
Bowl, 9"-10"	50	60	75					
Bowl, 5"	30	35	40					
Plate, 9"	80	90	135					
Vase, 7"-15", 2 Types	40	55	90	50			160W	500
Compote					165			
FISH NET (DUGAN)								
Epergne		450			475			
FISH VASE (CZECH)								
One shape, Marked "Jain"	450	400	500	450				

Field Flower

File

Fine Cut and Roses

Fine Prisms and Diamonds

20

Fleur De Lis (Czech)

Floral and Grape

Floral and Wheat

Flower Pot

	M	A	G	B	PO	AO	Pas	R
FISHERMAN'S MUG (DUGAN)								
One Size	400	210		550	1,450		255LV	
FISHSCALE AND BEADS (DUGAN)								
Bowl, 6"-8"	35	45			150		70	
Bride's Basket, Complete					140			
Plate, 7"............................	50	200			185			
FIVE HEARTS (DUGAN)								
Bowl, Dome Base, 8¼"	95	110			165			
FIVE LILY EPERGNE								
Complete, Metal Fittings	175	250						
FIVE PANEL								
Candy Jar, Stemmed	70							
FLANNEL FLOWER (CRYSTAL)								
Compote, Large	120	155						
Cake Stand........................	140	195						
FLARED PANEL								
Shade..............................					75MO			
FLARED WIDE PANEL								
Atomizer, 3½".....................	90							
FLEUR-DE-LIS (CZECH)								
Vase	1,100							
FLEUR-DE-LIS (MILLERSBURG)								
Bowl, Flat, 8½"	240	350	300				240CM	
Bowl, Ftd, 8½"	260	370	400					
Compote, Very Rare			5,000*					
Rose Bowl, Either Base, Rare ...		4,500						
FLICKERING FLAMES								
Shade..............................							50	
FLORA (ENGLISH)								
Float Bowl				90				
FLORABELLE								
Pitcher.............................							600IG	
Tumbler							200IG	
FLORAL								
Hatpin..............................							75AM	
FLORAL FAN								
Etched Vase.......................	57							
FLORAL AND GRAPE (DUGAN)								
Pitcher.............................	145	200		185			450W	
Tumbler	20	30		50			50W	
Hat, Whimsey.....................	40							
FLORAL AND GRAPE VT. (FENTON)								
Pitcher, 2 Variations	195	285	290	270				
Tumbler	30	35	40	30				
FLORAL AND OPTIC (IMPERIAL)								
Bowl, Ftd, 8"-10"	35				150		40SM	400
Bowl, Flat, 8"-10"	30						20SM	
Cake Plate, Ftd					180		50SM	650
Rose Bowl, Ftd					190		185AQ	
FLORAL OVAL (HIG-BEE)								
Bowl, 8"............................	50							
Plate, 7", Rare....................	90							
Creamer	60							
FLORAL AND SCROLL								
Shade, Various Shapes	45							
FLORAL SUNBURST								
Vase	175							
FLORAL AND WHEAT (DUGAN)								
Compote............................	40	45		45	150			
Bon-bon, Stemmed..............	40	45		45	155			
FLORENTINE (FENTON AND NORTHWOOD								
Candlesticks, pair...............	120		160RG	150CeB			140IG	1,050
FLORENTINE (IMPERIAL)								
Hat Vase............................							95	
FLOWER BASKET								
One Size............................	50							
FLOWER AND BEADS								
Plate, 6 Sided, 7½"..............	95	115						
Plate, Round, 8½"	95							
FLOWER MEDALLION								
Tumbler, very rare	800							
FLOWER POT (FENTON)								
One Size, Complete..............	60							
FLOWERING DILL (FENTON)								
Hat....................................	40		45	40			75	550
FLOWERING VINE (MILLERSBURG)								
Compote, Tall, Very Rare		4,200	4,200					

Flute (Millersburg)

Flute #3

Footed Prism Panels

Formal

	M	A	G	B	PO	AO	Pas	R
FLOWERS AND FRAMES (DUGAN)								
Bowl, 8"-10"	70	200	85		300		95	
FLOWERS AND SPADES (DUGAN)								
Bowl, 10".............................	50	90	85		210			
Bowl, 5"...............................	25	40	37		80			
FLUTE (BRITISH)								
Sherbet, Marked "British"....	50							
FLUTE (MILLERSBURG)								
Vase, Rare	300	400	425					
Bowl, 4" (Variant)................		45						
Compote, 6" (Marked "Krystol," Very Rare)..............	450	500						
Punch Bowl and Base, Rare.	265	320						
Punch Cup	27	30						
Bowl, 10".............................	65	90						
Bowl, 5"..............................	25	40						
FLUTE (NORTHWOOD)								
Creamer or Sugar	75	85	95					
Salt Dip, Ftd.......................	32						75V	
Sherbet	35	50	45				55CeB	
Pitcher, Rare......................	395		600					
Tumbler, 3 Varieties.............	50							
Ringtree, Rare	175							
Bowl, 10".............................	45	55						
Bowl, 5"..............................	25	30						
Butter	135	170	185					
FLUTE #3 (IMPERIAL)								
Covered Butter	180	240	210					
Sugar, Creamer or Spooner..............................	90	105	95					
Celery, Rare........................		390						
Punch Bowl and Base..........	295	500	470					
Punch Cup	25	40	38					
Pitcher................................	300	595	510	450				
Tumbler	40	195	185	100			300AQ	300
Handled Toothpick Holder ...	85							
Toothpick Holder, Regular ...	70	65	75	95			300AQ	
Bowl, 10"..............................		225						
Bowl, 5"..............................	30	70						
Custard Bowl, 11"		300	300					
Cruet..................................	90							
FLUTE AND CANE (IMPERIAL)								
Pitcher, Stemmed, Rare	400							
Wine...................................	50							
Champagne, Rare................	135							
Milk Pitcher........................	115							
Punch Cup	25							
Tumbler, Rare	450							
FLUTED SCROLL (DUGAN)								
Rose Bowl, Ftd, Very Rare....		975						
FLYING BAT								
Hatpin, Scarce....................	195	200	200				350	
FOLDING FAN (DUGAN)								
Compote.............................		75		85	120	295		
FOOTED DRAPE (WESTMORELAND)								
Vase	50						55W	
FOOTED PRISM PANELS (ENGLISH)								
Vase	85		120	100				
FOOTED RIB (NORTHWOOD)								
Vase	50	80	90	75		190	110	
Vase, Advertising						250	150	
FOOTED SHELL (WESTMORELAND)								
Large, 5"............................	40	50	55	55			75AM	
Small, 3"	45	55	60	60	100MO		70AM	
FORGET-ME-NOT (FENTON)								
Pitcher...............................	165	285	300	320			350W	
Tumbler	30	40	50	45			55W	
FORKS (CAMBRIDGE)								
Cracker Jar, Rare			500					
FORMAL (DUGAN)								
Hatpin Holder, Rare............	175	170						
Vase, Jack-In-Pulpit, Rare ...	125	100					150	
49'ER (IMPERIAL)								
Tumbler	75							
Wine...................................	80							
Decanter	125							
Pitcher, Squat.....................	210							
FOSTORIA #600 (FOSTORIA)								
Napkin Ring	75							
FOSTORIA #1231 (FOSTORIA)								
Rose Bowl...........................							145	

Four Flowers Variant

French Knots

Frolicking Bears

Fruits and Flowers

	M	A	G	B	PO	AO	Pas	R
FOSTORIAL #1299 (FOSTORIA)								
Tumbler	150*							
FOUNTAIN LAMP								
Complete, Scarce................	290							
FOUR FLOWERS								
Plate, 6½"		210	200		290			
Plate, 9"-10½"		700			560			
Rose Bowl, Rare		850*						
Bowl, 6¼"		45	50	70	190			
Bowl, 10"		180	185	190	220			
FOUR FLOWERS VT.								
Bowl, 9"-11"	70	75	70		210		170LV	
Bowl, Ftd, 8½"		80	90					
Plate, 10½", Rare		450	470				400TL	
Bowl on Metal Base, Rare		350LV			300		350TL	
FOUR PILLARS (NORTHWOOD AND DUGAN)								
Vase	50	60	75	60	110	175	75CT	
474 (IMPERIAL)								
Bowl, 8"-9"	60		85					
Punch Bowl and Base..........	220	700	600					
Cup..	30	40	35					
Covered Butter	100	150	125					
Creamer, Sugar or Spooner........................	65	90	85					
Milk Pitcher, Scarce.............	225		475				600LV	
Pitcher, 2 Sizes, Scarce........	210	510	480				610PK	
Tumbler, Scarce	35	80	65				120PK	
Goblet	50	90	65					
Wine..........................	75							
Cordial, Rare	90	210						
Vase, 7", Rare								3,200
Vase, 14", Rare	950		1,100					
FRENCH KNOTS (FENTON)								
Hat......................................	40	50	50	45				
FRENCH GRAPE								
Bowl, 4"..............................	175							
FROLICKING BEADS (U.S. GLASS)								
Pitcher, Rare........................		10,000						
Tumbler, Rare		8,000						
FROSTED BLOCK (IMPERIAL)								
Bowl, 6½"-7½".......................	30						35CM	
Bowl, 9"..............................	35						40CM	
Celery Tray..........................	40							
Covered Butter	70							
Creamer or Sugar	50							
Rose Bowl..........................	50						75CM	
Compote.............................	85						120CM	
Milk Pitcher, Rare	90							
Pickle Dish, Handled, Rare ..	60						65CM	
Bowl, Square, Rare	50						60CM	
Plate, 7½"	70						65CM	
Plate, 9"..............................							170CM	
Vase, 6"							100SM	
25% More if Marked "Made in USA"								
FROSTED BUTTONS (FENTON)								
Bowl, Ftd, 10".....................							175	
FROSTED RIBBON								
Pitcher................................	85							
Tumbler	30							
FROSTY								
Bottle	30							
FRUIT BASKET (MILLERSBURG)								
Compote, Handled, Rare......		1,950						
FRUIT AND BERRIES (ENGLISH)								
Bean Pot, Covered, Rare	385			425				
FRUIT AND FLOWERS (NORTHWOOD)								
Bowl, 9"...............................	100	150	140				250	
Bowl, 5"...............................	40	50	55				75	
Fruit Bowl, 10"	110	170					80	
Banana Plate, 7", Rare........		350	325					
Bon-bon, Stemmed..............	60	100	85	275		380	350W	
Plate, 7"...............................	185	250	195	240				
Plate, 9½"	235	270	260				385	
FRUIT JAR (BALL)								
One Size	65							
FRUIT LUSTRE								
Tumbler	40							
FRUIT SALAD (WESTMORELAND)								
Punch Bowl and Base, Rare ...	600	700			3,900			
Cup, Rare............................	30	40			60			

Garden Mums

Garland

Golden Grape

Golden Honeycomb

	M	A	G	B	PO	AO	Pas	R
GAMBIER, MT, (CRYSTAL)								
Mug	95							
GARDEN MUMS (NORTHWOOD)								
Bowl, 8½"-10"	60	75	80	85			110	
Plate, Regular or Handgrip, 7"	180	210	225	240			250	
Shallow Bowl, 5"		200						
GARDEN PATH (DUGAN)								
Bowl, 8½"-10"	60	85		140				
Compote, Rare	200	365					500	
Fruit Bowl, 10"	90	115						
Plate, 6", Rare	430	585			985			
Bowl, 5"					60			
GARDEN PATH VT. (DUGAN)								
Bowl, 9"					175			
Fruit Bowl, 10"		375			410			
Plate, 11", Rare		10,465			3,300			
Rose Bowl, Rare	400							
GARLAND (FENTON)								
Rose Bowl, Ftd	55	70		60				
GAY 90'S (MILLERSBURG)								
Pitcher, Rare		8,500	9,500					
Tumbler, Rare	1,250	1,150						
GEO. GETZ PIANOS (NORTHWOOD)								
Plate		2,000						
GEORGIA BELLE (DUGAN)								
Compote, Ftd	65	75	85		140			
Card Tray, Ftd, Rare	75	80	95		175			
GERVUTZ BROTHERS (NORTHWOOD)								
Bowl		750						
GOD AND HOME (DUGAN)								
Pitcher, Rare				2,000				
Tumbler, Rare				275				
GODDESS ATHENA								
Epergne, Rare			2,000				2,000AM	
GODDESS OF HARVEST (FENTON)								
Bowl, 9½", Rare	6,000	6,900		6,500				
Plate, Very Rare		7,800						
GOLD FISH								
Bowl	145							
GOLDEN CUPIDS (CRYSTAL)								
Bowl, 9", Rare							500	
Bowl, 5", Rare							225	
GOLDEN FLOWERS								
Vase, 7½"	95							
GOLDEN GRAPES (DUGAN)								
Bowl, 7"	35	45	60				50	
Rose Bowl, Collar Base	85							
GOLDEN HARVEST (U.S. GLASS)								
Decanter w/stopper	125	250						
Wine	25	35						
GOLDEN HONEYCOMB (IMPERIAL)								
Bowl, 5"	25							
Plate, 7"	55							
Compote	50							
Creamer or Sugar	35							
Bon-bon	45	55	60				60AM	
GOLDEN OXEN								
Mug	90							
GOLDEN WEDDING								
Bottle, Various Sizes	40+							
GOOD LUCK (NORTHWOOD)								
Bowl, 8¼"	235	400	475	450		1,300	4,200IB	
Plate, 9"	425+	700+	850+	1,100+			5000IB	
GOOD LUCK VT. (NORTHWOOD)								
Bowl, 8¼", Rare	300	400	450				600	
GOODYEAR								
Ashtray in Tire	60							
GOOSEBERRY SPRAY								
Bowl, 10"	55	85	90	90			120	
Bowl, 5"		110	125	125			155	
Compote, Rare		225	260	250			260	
GOTHIC ARCHES								
Vase, 8"-12", Rare	45	70	85	95			95SM	
GRACEFUL (NORTHWOOD)								
Vase	60	100	120	135			200W	
GRACEFUL TUMBLER								
Tumbler				800			500AMB	

Grape and Cable (Fenton)

Grape (Imperial)

Grape and Cable (Northwood)

	M	A	G	B	PO	AO	Pas	R
GRAND THISTLE (FINLAND)								
Pitcher, Rare..............				1,900				
Tumbler, Rare				400				
GRAPE (FENTON'S								
GRAPE AND CABLE)								
Orange Bowl, Ftd..............	110	220	240	200			265	
Orange Bowl, Advertising,								
Very Rare.....................	1,900			2,200				
Bowl, Ftd, 8¾"..................	65	80	95	775				
Bowl, Flat, 8"...................	50	60	80	70		850	600	900
Plate, Ftd, 9"...................	145	350	200					1,600
Orange Basket, Very Rare....		3,800						
Spittoon Whimsey, Rare	1,150							
GRAPE (IMPERIAL)								
Bowl, 10".......................	40	80	65				135AM	
Bowl, 5"..........................	25	40	30				40SM	
Fruit Bowl, 8¾".................	40	60	55					365
Compote..........................	50	60	60				275SM	
Cup and Saucer	70	155	50					
Nappy............................	30		40				35SM	
Tray, Center Handle	45						65HA	
Goblet, Rare	40	75	65				70AM	
Plate, 7"-12"	90	290	175	1,750			150AM	
Plate, Ruffled, 8½"	45	65	50	55			70SM	
Pitcher............................	100	350	175				270SM	
Tumbler..........................	25	45	30				40SM	
Punch Bowl and Base.........	135	390	275				300SM	
Cup................................	20	45	35				30AM	
Water Bottle, Rare	125	250	165				270CM	
Milk Pitcher.......................	260	350	300				190CM	
Basket, Handled, Rare..........	75		90				130SM	
Rose Bowl, Rare	175	225	190					
Decanter w/stopper.............	135	270	170				150	
Wine................................	30	40	35				90SM	
Spittoon Whimsey................	1,100		2,250					
GRAPE (NORTHWOOD'S								
GRAPE AND CABLE)								
Bowl, Flat, 9"-10"	200	75	85	75		3,200		
Bowl, Flat, 5½"							75W	
Scalloped Bowl, 5½"-11½"	80+	75+	100+	120			750IG	
Bon-bon	65	58	105	100			350W	
Banana Boat, Ftd	250	300	400	425			700IB	
Bowl, Ftd..........................	60	80	105	90				
Ice Cream Bowl, 11"	150	325	350	500		1700	400IB	
Orange Bowl, Ftd.................		250		450				
Breakfast Set, 2 pcs.............	140	250	200					
Candlelamp, Complete.........	800	475	500					
Compote, Covered	2,500	350						
Compote, Open..................	500	375	1,100				750	
Sweetmeat w/lid.................	1,850	165		2,000				
Sweetmeat Whimsey...........	400	325						
Cookie Jar w/lid.................	350	500				9,000	2,350IG	
Centerpiece Bowl, Ftd.........	300	595	1,100	1,250			1,100IG	
Cup and Saucer, Rare.........	400	425						
Cologne w/stopper	180	195	220				600IB	
Perfume w/stopper..............	375	650						
Dresser Tray......................	175	250	295				550IB	
Pin Tray	395	195	250				250IC	
Hatpin Holder.....................	275	300	275	900		12,000	2,000W	
Powder Jar w/lid	100	150	180	200				
Nappy..............................	85	100	135	165				
Fernery, Rare	1,250	950	1,000				1,200W	
Hat..................................	40	50	50				90	
Ice Cream Sherbet	40	50	60				90	
Plate, Flat, 6"-9½"	150	200	250	750			2,000TL	
Plate, Handgrip...................	140	200	220				240	
Plate, Ftd..........................	65	95	110	135			1,200IG	
Plate, 2 Sides Up	200	170	375					
Shade..............................	200	180						
Punch Bowl and Base								
(Standard)	380	500	500	900			900	
Punch Bowl and Base (Small) ..	300	600	700	850			10,000IB	
Plate, Advertising.................			375					
Punch Bowl and Base								
(Banquet)	2,000	2,300	3,000	4,200			16,000IB	
Cup..................................	25	27	50	60			80W	
Butter	175	220	225				300	
Sugar w/lid	70	85	85				150	
Creamer or Spooner	45	85	75					
Tobacco Jar w/lid................	350	525		1,350				
Pitcher, Standard.................	270	250	300				2,000IG	
Pitcher, Tankard.................	700	800	3,300				2,600IG	
Tumbler, Jumbo	60	75	90					
Tumbler, Regular.................	50	60	75				500IG	
Decanter w/stopper.............	650	700						
Shot Glass.........................	125	285						
Spittoon, Rare	6,000	7,800	7,500					

Grape Arbor (Northwood)

Grapevine Lattice

Hammered Bell

Harvest Flower

	M	A	G	B	PO	AO	Pas	R
Grape (Northwood's Grape and Cable) Cont'd								
Orange Bowl, Blackberry Interior, Rare		1,800						
Hatpin Holder Whimsey, Rare .		3,500	4,000					
GRAPE ARBOR (DUGAN)								
Bowl, Ftd, 9½"-11"	150	400					150W	
GRAPE ARBOR (NORTHWOOD)								
Pitcher................................	320	650		3,000			550W	
Tumbler	45	70		375			400IG	
Hat.......................................	75			175			350IG	
GRAPE AND CHERRY (ENGLISH)								
Bowl, 8½", Rare	75			180				
GRAPE DELIGHT (DUGAN)								
Rose Bowl, Ftd, 6"	65	80		70			70W	
Nut Bowl, Ftd, 6"	65	120		180			80W	
GRAPE FIEZE (NORTHWOOD)								
Bowl, 10½", Rare							600IC	
GRAPE AND GOTHIC ARCHES (NORTHWOOD)								
Bowl, 10"	80	120	90	80	150PL			
Bowl, 5"	25	40	40	35	45PL			
Butter	100	140	140	125	420PL			
Sugar w/lid	75	120	110	90	125PL			
Creamer or Spooner	55	85	75	70	125PL			
Pitcher.................................	200	385	400	360	750PL			
Tumbler	35	80	70	50	170PL		160CM	
GRAPE, HEAVY (DUGAN)								
Bowl, 5", Rare.....................	160	185			395			
Bowl, 10", ...	240	295			600			
GRAPE, HEAVY (IMPERIAL)								
Bowl, 9"	45	65						
Bowl, 5"	25	30						
Nappy...................................	45	55						
Plate, 8"	65	85	90				200AM	
Plate, 6"	52	60	70				90	
Plate, 11"	265	375					350IG	
Fruit Bowl w/base	295							
Custard Cup	20	35	35					
Punch Bowl w/base.............	210	510	450					
GRAPE LEAVES (MILLERSBURG)								
Bowl, 10", Rare....................	600	800	900				850V	
GRAPE LEAVES (NORTHWOOD)								
Bowl, 8¼"	65	80	85	90			450IB	
Brides Basket, Complete......		300						
GRAPE WREATH (MILLERSBURG)								
Bowl, 5"	40	55	320					
Bowl, 7½"-9"	60	75	80	420				
Bowl, Ice Cream, 10"	120	175	175					
Spittoon Whimsey, Rare	3,200		3,800					
GRAPEVINE LATTICE (DUGAN)								
Bowl, 8½"	42	60	52	65			80W	
Plate, 7"-9"	75	95		90			150W	
Bowl, 5"	30						60W	
Hat Shape, Jip.....................	75							
GRAPEVINE LATTICE (FENTON)								
Pitcher, Rare.......................	325	600		650			850W	
Tumbler, Rare	55	75		95			100W	
GREEK KEY (NORTHWOOD)								
Bowl, 7"-8½"	90	120	150	375				
Plate, 9"-11", Rare	1,050	850	1,200	2,900		1,750*		
Pitcher, Rare.......................	450	900	1,650					
Tumbler, Rare	85	195	210					
GREEK KEY VT.								
Hatpin..................................		90						
GREENGARD FURNITURE (MILLERSBURG)								
Bowl, Rare...........................		1,295						
HAIR RECEIVER								
Complete	75							
HAMMERED BELL CHANDELIER								
Complete, 5 Shades.............							600W	
Shade, Each							95W	
HAND VASE								
One Shape, 5½"-8"................	180	280						450*
HANDLED TUMBLER								
One Size	55							
HANDLED VASE (IMPERIAL)								
One Shape............................	47							
HARVEST FLOWER (DUGAN)								
Pitcher, Rare.......................	1,250							
Tumbler	105	300	365					
HARVEST POPPY								
Compote................................	320			450				

Heron

Heart and Flowers

Heavy Prisms

	M	A	G	B	PO	AO	Pas	R
HATCHET (U.S. GLASS)								
One Shape	150							
HATTIE (IMPERIAL)								
Bowl	47	115						
Rose Bowl	95						250AM	
Plate, Rare	875	700	500				900	
HAWAIIAN LEI (HIGBEE)								
Sugar	75							
Creamer	75							
HAWAIIAN MOON								
Pitcher	200						250CRAN	
Tumbler	75						90CRAN	
HEADDRESS								
Bowl, 9", 2 Varieties	47		60	52				
Compote	58		75	60				
HEART BAND								
One Shape (Salt)	45							
HEART BAND SOUVENIR (McKEE)								
Mug, Small	85		100				115AQ	
Mug, Large	90		115				127AQ	
HEART AND HORSESHOE (FENTON)								
Bowl, 8½"	900							
Plate, 9", Rare	1,150							
HEART AND TREES (FENTON)								
Bowl, 8¾"	165		215	200				
HEART AND VINE (FENTON)								
Bowl, 8½"	80	50	115	120			70LV	
Plate, 9", Rare	300	475	365	350				
Spector Plate, Advertising, Rare	900							
HEARTS AND FLOWERS (NORTHWOOD)								
Bowl, 8½"	525	450	750	650			1,200IG	
Compote	300	550	2,400	500		800	900IG	
Plate, 9", Rare	1,000	1,150	1,850	550		2,300	1,350IB	
HEAVY DIAMOND								
Nappy	40							
HEAVY DIAMOND (IMPERIAL)								
Bowl, 10"	45							
Creamer	30							
Sugar	35							
Vase	50		65				85SM	
Compote	45		55					
HEAVY HEART (HIGBEE)								
Tumbler	150							
HEAVY HOBNAIL (FENTON)								
Vase, Rare		550					465W	
HEAVY HOBS								
Lamp (Amber Base Glass)					300			
HEAVY PRISMS (ENGLISH)								
Celery Vase, 6"	85	115		95				
HEAVY SHELL (FENTON)								
Bowl, 8¼"							150	
Candleholder, Each							100	
HEAVY VINE								
Lamp	250							
Atomizer	85							
HEAVY WEB (DUGAN)								
Bowl, 10", Rare					1,300			
Plate, 11", Rare					1,800			
HEINZ								
Bottle							58	
HEISEY								
Breakfast Set							290	
HEISEY CARTWHEEL								
Compote							85	
HEISEY FLORAL SPRAY								
Stemmed Candy w/lid, 11"							85IB	
HEISEY FLUTE								
Punch Cup	35							
HEISEY SET								
Creamer and Tray	150						195	
HEISEY #357								
Water Bottle	190							
Tumbler	65							
HERON (DUGAN)								
Mug, Rare	1,000	375						
HERRINGBONE AND BEADED OVAL								
Compote, Rare	600*							

	M	A	G	B	PO	AO	Pas	R
HERRINGBONE AND MUMS (JEANETTE)								
Tumbler, very rare	600							
HEXAGON AND CANE (IMPERIAL)								
Covered Sugar	90							
HEX BASE								
Candlesticks, pair...............	75	125	110				175SM	
HEX-OPTIC (JEANETTE)								
Pitcher..............................							135CL	
Tumbler							50CL	
HICKMAN								
Castor Set, 4 pc....................	250						450	
HOBNAIL (FENTON)								
Vase, 5"-11"......................							95+W	
HOBNAIL (MILLERSBURG)								
Pitcher, Rare......................	1,800	1,900	2,200	1,600				
Tumbler, Rare	775	500	1,000	950				
Rose Bowl, Scarce	200	395	595					
Spittoon, Rare	900	1,000	1,800					
Butter, Rare.......................	500	600	650	800				
Sugar w/lid, Rare	350	500	575	800				
Creamer or Spooner, Rare....	275	375	450	500				
HOBNAIL VT. (MILLERSBURG)								
Vase Whimsey, Rare	600	750	750					
Rose Bowl, Rare	900							
Jardinere, Rare...................		950		1,100				
HOBNAIL, MINIATURE								
Tumbler, 2½"	50							
Pitcher 6", Rare	250							
HOBNAIL PANELS (McKEE)								
Vase, 8¾"............................							70CM	
HOBNAIL SODA GOLD (IMPERIAL)								
Spittoon, Large	50		75				60W	
HOBSTAR (IMPERIAL)								
Bowl, Berry, 10"	40						50	
Bowl, Berry, 5"	25						35	
Bowls, Various								
Shapes, 6"-12"...................	30						40	
Fruit Bowl w/base..............	50	85	75					
Cookie Jar w/lid.................	65		100					
Butter	80	195	185				90CM	
Sugar w/lid	65	100	90				60CM	
Creamer or Spooner	45	85	75				50CM	
Pickle Castor, Complete	450							
Bride's Basket, Complete.....	75							
Vase, Flared.......................	350	200						
HOBSTAR AND ARCHES (IMPERIAL)								
Bowl, 9"............................	50	75	60				60SM	
Fruit Bowl w/base..............	60	90	75					
HOBSTAR BAND (IMPERIAL)								
Celery................................	85							
Compote, Rare....................	100							
Bowl, Rare.........................	90							
Pitcher, 2 Shapes, Rare.......	275							
Tumbler, 2 Shapes, Rare	70							
HOBSTAR AND WAFFLE BLOCK (IMPERIAL)								
Basket...............................	150						175SM	
HOBSTAR AND CUT TRIANGLES (ENGLISH)								
Rose Bowl..........................	45	55	70					
Bowl..................................	30	40	60					
Plate..................................	70	100	110					
HOBSTAR DIAMONDS								
Tumbler, very rare	500							
HOBSTAR AND FEATHER (MILLERSBURG)								
Punch Bowl and Base (Open), Rare	1,800		3,800					
Punch Bowl and Base (Tulip), Rare		3,500						
Punch Cup, Scarce	30	40		275*				
Rose Bowl, Giant, Rare	3,000*	2,000	2,000					
Vase Whimsey, Rare		5,000	5,000					
Punch Bowl Whimsey, Rare ...			7,500					
Compote Whimsey (From Rose Bowl), Rare..................		5,500						
Bowl, Round, 5", Rare		450						
Bowl, Diamond, 5", Rare......	400							
Bowl, Heart, 5", Rare	350							
Butter, Rare.......................	1,500	1,800	1,800					
Sugar w/lid, Rare	900	1,000	1,000					
Creamer, Rare	700	800	800					
Spooner, Rare.....................	700	800	800					
Dessert, Stemmed, Rare	650							
Compote, 6" Rare................	1,500							

Hobstar

Hobstar Band

Hobstar and Feather

Hobstar and Cut Triangles

Hobstar Whirl

Holly

Honeycomb and Clover

Honeycomb and Hobstar

	M	A	G	B	PO	AO	Pas	R
Hobstar and Feather (Millersburg) Cont.								
Stemmed Whimsey								
Tray-Ftd, 4½", Very Rare....	750							
HOBSTAR AND FILE								
Pitcher, Rare.......................	1,700							
Tumbler, Rare	200							
HOBSTAR FLOWER (NORTHWOOD)								
Compote, Scarce.................	55	65	70	80				
HOBSTAR AND FRUIT (WESTMORELAND)								
Bowl, 6", Rare.....................					100	300		
Bowl, 10", Rare...................					195			
Plate, 10½", Rare							400IB	
HOBSTAR PANELS (ENGLISH)								
Creamer	45							
Sugar, Stemmed	45							
HOBSTAR REVERSED (ENGLISH)								
Spooner..............................	45							
Butter	55	75		70				
Frog and Holder	50							
HOBSTAR WHIRL (WHIRLAGIG)								
Compote, 4½"	50	60		60				
HOLIDAY								
Bottle							75	
HOLIDAY (NORTHWOOD)								
Tray, 11", Rare...................	375							
HOLLY (FENTON)								
Bowl, 8"-10"	75	80	90	90			150W	1,400
Compote, 5"........................	45	50	85	50			85AM	1,100
Goblet	40	60		60			90W	600
Hat.....................................	35	40	50	40			75LG	450
Plate, 9".............................	280	300	450	345			850BA	2,800
Rose Bowl...........................	400		900*	500				
HOLLY AND BERRY (DUGAN)								
Bowl, 7"-9"	40	47	50	50	70			
Nappy.................................	45	55	60	55	70			
Gravy Boat, Handled		65		65	140			
HOLLY, PANELLED (NORTHWOOD)								
Bowl....................................		75	70					
Bon-bon, Ftd	60	90	75					
Creamer or Sugar	90							
Pitcher, Rare.......................		12,000*						
Spooner...............................	50							
HOLLY SPRIG VT. (MILLERSBURG)								
Bowl, Scarce.......................	290	320	350					
HOLLY SPRIG OR WHIRL (MILLERSBURG)								
Deep Sauce, Rare	175	275	350					
Nappy, Tri-Cornered, Rare...	85	115	120					
Bon-bon (Plain)...................	55	60	60					
Bon-bon (Isaac Benesch), Rare	125							
Bowl, Round or Ruffled, 7"-10"....................	50	65	60				60CM	
Compote, Very Rare	450	625					1,000V	
Rose Bowl Whimsey, Rare....							1,250V	
Bowl, Tri-Cornered, 7"-10"...	325	200	190					
HOLLOWEEN								
Pitcher, 2 sizes	485							
Tumbler, 2 sizes	175							
Spittoon	600							
HOLM SPRAY								
Atomizer, 3"........................	65							
HOMESTEAD								
Shade.................................	50							
HONEYBEE (JEANETTE)								
Pot							85	
HONEYCOMB (DUGAN)								
Rose Bowl...........................	190				250			
HONEYCOMB AND CLOVER (FENTON)								
Bon-bon	40	60	60	50			70AM	
Compote..............................	35	50	60	50				
Spooner, Rare.....................	95							
HONEYCOMB AND HOBSTAR (MILLERSBURG)								
Vase, 8¼", Rare...................		7,000		7,500				
HONEYCOMB ORNAMENT								
Hatpin................................		80		90				

Horseshoe Shot Glass

Illinois Daisy

Imperial Paperweight

Intaglio Daisy

	M	A	G	B	PO	AO	Pas	R
HONEYCOMB PANELS								
Tumbler		175*						
HORN OF PLENTY								
Bottle	60							
HORN, POWDER (CAMBRIDGE)								
Candy Holder	200							
HORSES HEADS (FENTON)								
Bowl, Flat, 7½"	75		325	250			290W	1,200
Bowl, Ftd, 7"-8"	95		335	270			295W	1,200
Plate, 6½"-8½"	310			800				
Rose Bowl, Ftd	260			400			800V	
Nut Bowl, Rare		250						
HORSESHOE								
Shot Glass.........................	50							
HOT SPRINGS SOUVENIR								
Vase, 9⅞", Rare...................	115*							
HOURGLASS								
Bud Vase...........................	50							
HUMPTY-DUMPTY								
Mustard Jar	75							
HYACINTH								
Lamp...............................	1,900							
ICE CRYSTALS								
Bowl, Ftd..........................							85	
Candlesticks, pair...............							160	
Salt, Ftd							65	
IDYLL (FENTON)								
Vase, Rare	550	750		850				
ILLINOIS DAISY (ENGLISH)								
Bowl, 8"............................	40							
Cookie Jar w/lid..................	60							
ILLUSION (FENTON)								
Bon-bon	55			85				
Bowl................................	60			90				
IMPERIAL BASKET (IMPERIAL)								
One Shape, Rare	65						80	
IMPERIAL DAISY (IMPERIAL)								
Shade...............................	45							
IMPERIAL GRAPE (IMPERIAL)								
Shade...............................	85							
IMPERIAL #5 (IMPERIAL)								
Bowl, 8"............................	40							
Vase, 6", Rare	95						50AM	
IMPERIAL #9 (IMPERIAL)								
Compote............................	40							
IMPERIAL PAPERWEIGHT (IMPERIAL)								
Advertising Weight, Rare......		1,050						
INCA								
Vase, 7", Rare	900	950						
Bottle	175*							
INDIAN CANOE								
Novelty Boat Shape..............	100							
INDIANA GOBLET (INDIANA GLASS)								
One Shape, Rare							800AM	
INDIANA STATEHOUSE (FENTON)								
Plate, Rare.........................	2,900			3,500				
INSULATOR (VARIOUS MAKERS)								
Various Sizes......................	35+							
INTAGLIO DAISY (ENGLISH)								
Bowl, 7½"	50							
Bowl, 4½"	30							
INTAGLIO FEATHERS								
Cup.................................	25							
INTAGLIO OVALS (U.S. GLASS)								
Bowl, 7"............................						70		
Plate, 7½"						90		
INTAGLIO STARS								
Tumbler, Rare	600							
INTERIOR PANELS								
Mug.................................	75							
INTERIOR POINSETTIA (NORTHWOOD)								
Tumbler, Rare	485							
INTERIOR RAYS								
Sherbet	35							
INTERIOR RAYS (WESTMORELAND)								
Covered Butter	65							
Sugar, Creamer or Jam Jar, Each...........................	40							
INTERIOR SWIRL								
Vase, Ftd, 9"	40							
Spittoon					95			

	M	A	G	B	PO	AO	Pas	R
INVERTED COIN DOT (NORTHWOOD-FENTON)								
Pitcher............................	325	450		400				
Tumbler	75	95		85				
Bowl................................	40	50	70	50			70	
Rose Bowl.........................	50		60				85	
INVERTED FEATHER (CAMBRIDGE)								
Cracker Jar w/lid		1,000	395					
Covered Butter, Rare	450	500						
Sugar, Creamer or Spooner, Rare.....................	400	325						
Pitcher, Tall, Rare	4,500							
Tumbler, Rare	500		600					
Compote............................	85							
Punch Bowl w/base, Rare....	3,000		4,000					
Cup, Rare..........................	60							
Wine, Rare.........................	200							
Squat Pitcher, Rare.............	1,200							
INVERTED STRAWBERRY								
Bowl, 9"-10½"	190	300	295	350				
Bowl, 5"..............................	40	55	50					
Sugar, Creamer or Spooner, Rare, Each	100			150				
Covered Butter		750						
Candlesticks, Rare, Pair	300	425	400					
Compote, Large, Rare	350	500	450					
Compote, Small, Rare	400			350				
Cruet Whimsey, Very Rare ...	1,500*							
Powder Jar, Rare	195							
Ladies Spittoon, Rare	900	1,000	1,000					
Milk Pitcher, Rare		1,850						
Pitcher, Rare......................	2,200	3,200	3,000					
Tumbler, Rare	300	250	350					
Table Set, 2 pcs, Rare (Stemmed)		1,275						
Celery, Rare.......................		1,300	1,300	1,300				
Compote Whimsey, Rare......	500							
INVERTED, THISTLE (CAMBRIDGE)								
Bowl, 9", Rare.....................		350	350					
Spittoon, Rare		4,000						
Covered Box, Rare				400				
Pitcher, Rare......................	3,800	3,500						
Tumbler, Rare	425	300						
Butter, Rare.......................	500	600	700					
Sugar, Creamer or Spooner, Rare	350	400	500					
Chop Plate, Rare..................		2,600						
Milk Pitcher, Rare		2,850						
Bowl, 5", Rare.....................		200	200					
IOWA								
Small Mug, Rare..................	95							
IRIS (FENTON)								
Compote............................	50	60	60	75			275W	
Buttermilk Goblet, Scarce	55	65	65				80AM	
IRIS, HEAVY (DUGAN)								
Pitcher...............................	400	750			1,000		1,200W	
Tumbler	90	80					150W	
IRIS HERRINGBONE (JEANETTE) Various Shapes, Prices range from $10.00 to $35.00 each in this late pattern.								
ISAAC BENESCH								
Advertising Bowl, 6½"		350						
Misspelled Version, Rare......		1050*						
I.W. HARPER								
Decanter w/stopper.............	85							
JACK-IN-THE-PULPIT (DUGAN)								
Vase	45	75		80	110			
JACKMAN								
Whiskey Bottle	50							
JACOB'S LADDER								
Perfume..............................	60							
JACOB'S LADDER VT. (U.S. GLASS)								
Rose Bowl............................	90							
JACOBEAN RANGER (CZECHOSLOVAKIAN AND ENGLISH)								
Pitcher...............................	350							
Tumbler	195							
Juice Tumbler	180							
Miniature Tumbler	350							
Decanter w/stopper.............	250							
Wine...................................	50							
Bowls, Various Sizes	60+							

Inverted Coin Dot

Isaac Benesch Bowl

Jack-in-the-Pulpit (Dugan)

Jackman Whiskey

Jelly Jar

Keyhole (Dugan)

Kingfisher Vt.

Lacy Dewdrop

	M	A	G	B	PO	AO	Pas	R
JARDINERE (FENTON)								
Various Shapes	350	500	500	600				
JELLY JAR								
Complete, Rare	65							
JEWEL BOX								
Ink Well	150							
JEWELED HEART (DUGAN)								
Bowl, 10"		95			135			
Bowl, 5"		40			65			
Pitcher, Rare	900							
Tumbler, Rare	100						575W	
Plate, 6"	195				250			
JEWELS (IMPERIAL — DUGAN)								
Candlesticks, Pair	90	150	180	190			120CeB	395
Bowls, Various Sizes		50	150	185			80	350
Hat Shape			65				90	300
Vase	100	150	150	175			195AM	250
Creamer or Sugar							70	235
JOCKEY CLUB (NORTHWOOD)								
Bowl, 7"		600						
KANGAROO (AUSTRALIAN)								
Bowl, 9½"	175	200						
Bowl, 5"	50	60						
KEYHOLE (DUGAN)								
Exterior Pattern of Raindrops Bowls								
KINGFISHER AND VARIANT (AUSTRALIAN)								
Bowl, 5"	50	60						
Bowl, 9½"	175	200						
KITTEN								
Miniature Paperweight, Rare	250							
KITTENS								
Bottle							65	
KITTENS (FENTON)								
Bowl, 4", Scarce				775			500AQ	
Bowl, 2 Sides Up, Scarce	175	500		625			500LV	
Cup and Saucer, Scarce	250			650				
Spooner, 2½", Rare	175			275			250V	
Plate, 4½", Scarce	175			250			275SM	
Cereal Bowl, Scarce	275			500				
Vase or Toothpick holder, 3"	175			400			300V	
Spittoon Whimsey, Rare	1,200			1,500*				
KIWI (AUSTRALIAN)								
Bowl, 10", Rare	350	300						
KNIGHT TEMPLAR (NORTHWOOD)								
Advertising Mug, Rare	600						1,200IG	
KNOTTED BEADS (FENTON)								
Vase, 4"-12"	30+		40+	40+			85V	
KOKOMO (ENGLISH)								
Rose Bowl, Ftd	45		60	50				
KOOKABURRA AND VTS. (AUSTRALIAN)								
Bowl, 5"	75	90						
Bowl, 10"	180	200						
LACY DEWDROP (WESTMORELAND)								
Pitcher							650	
Compote, Covered							350	
Bowl, Covered							280	
Banana Boat							375	
Tumbler							275	
Goblet							180	
Creamer							160	
Sugar							180	
(Note: All Items Listed Are in Pearl Carnival)								
LADY'S SLIPPER								
One Shape, Rare	250							
LARGE KANGAROO (AUSTRALIAN)								
Bowl, 5"	60	65						
Bowl, 10"	195	210						
LATE ENAMELED BLEEDING HEARTS								
Tumbler	175							
LATE ENAMELED GRAPE								
Goblet	90							
LATE ENAMELED STRAWBERRY								
Tumbler, tall	175							
LATTICE (DUGAN)								
Bowl, Various Sizes	60	70					85	

32

	M	A	G	B	PO	AO	Pas	R
LATTICE AND DAISY (DUGAN)								
Bowl, 9"	60							
Bowl, 5"	30							
Pitcher	225			285			325	
Tumbler	30	60		50			60	
LATTICE AND GRAPE (FENTON)								
Pitcher	260	425	485	410	2,200		850W	
Tumbler	38	45	55	40	500		300W	
Spittoon Whimsey, Rare	2,600							
LATTICE HEART (ENGLISH)								
Bowl, 10"	50	75		70				
Bowl, 5"	30			40				
Compote	60	90		85				
LATTICE AND LEAVES								
Vase, 9½"	275			295				
LATTICE AND POINTS (DUGAN)								
Vase	40	45					65W	
LATTICE AND PRISMS								
Cologne w/stopper	65							
LATTICE AND SPRAYS								
Vase, 10½"	50							
LAUREL								
Shade	40						50	
LAUREL BAND								
Tumbler	40							
LAUREL AND GRAPE								
Vase, 6"	120							
LAUREL LEAVES (IMPERIAL)								
Plate	40	55					60SM	
LBJ HAT								
Ashtray	35							
LEA AND VT. (ENGLISH)								
Bowl, Ftd	40							
Pickle Dish, Handled	45							
Creamer, Ftd	45	50						
LEAF AND BEADS (NORTHWOOD-DUGAN)								
Bowl, 9"	150	275	700			275		
Plate Whimsey	495*							
Candy Dish, Ftd	80	110	115			575	425	
Rose Bowl, Ftd	90	120	125	190		1,000	500W	
Nut Bowl, Rare						1,200		
(Note: Add 25% for Patterned Interior)								
LEAF CHAIN (FENTON)								
Bon-bon	40	55	60	50				
Bowl, 7"-9"	60	80	90	140		1,400	165W	750
Plate, 7½"	195			150				
Plate, 9¼"	460	150	175	135		2,350	225W	
LEAF COLUMN (NORTHWOOD)								
Vase	30	45	45		150		190IB	
Shade							90	
LEAF AND LITTLE FLOWERS (MILLERSBURG)								
Compote, Miniature, Rare	450	495	475					
LEAF RAYS (DUGAN)								
Nappy, Either Exterior	30	40			50		60W	
LEAF SWIRL (WESTMORELAND)								
Compote	55	75		65TL			70AM	
LEAF SWIRL AND FLOWER (FENTON)								
Vase	55						65W	
LEAF TIERS (FENTON)								
Bowl, Ftd, 10"	60							
Bowl, Ftd, 5"	30							
Butter, Ftd	175							
Sugar, Ftd	90							
Creamer, Spooner, Ftd	85							
Pitcher, Ftd, Rare	475	650	650	695				
Tumbler, Ftd, Rare	75	90	90	95				
Banana Bowl Whimsey	200							
LIGHTNING FLOWER								
Nappy, Rare	450*							
LILY OF THE VALLEY (FENTON)								
Pitcher, Rare				3,900				
Tumbler, Rare	700			450				
LINED LATTICE (DUGAN)								
Vase, 7"-14"	40	110	90	80	160		60W	
Hat Shape	40							
LION (FENTON)								
Bowl, 7", Scarce	115			160				
Plate, 7½", Rare	900							

Lattice and Daisy

Leaf Chain

Leaf Column

Leaf Rays

Little Daisies

Little Stars

Long Hobstar

Long Thumbprint

	M	A	G	B	PO	AO	Pas	R
LITTLE BARREL (IMPERIAL)								
One Shape......................	175		195				210AM	
LITTLE BEADS								
Bowl, 8"......................	22				45			
Compote, Small..................	30				50	95	40AQ	
LITTLE DAISIES (FENTON)								
Bowl, 8"-9½", Rare..............	395			475				
LITTLE DAISY								
Lamp, Complete, 8".............							500	
LITTLE DARLING								
Bottle......................	60							
LITTLE FISHES (FENTON)								
Bowl, Flat or Ftd, 10"...........	250		340	365			1,100W	
Bowl Flat or Ftd, 5½", ...	75	290	280	185			350W	
Plate, 10½", Rare				850			1,350W	
LITTLE FLOWERS (FENTON)								
Bowl, 9¼"	65	100	115	135			140AM	11,000
Bowl, 5½", Rare	40	80	70	75			80V	
Plate, 7", Rare	245							
Plate, 10", Rare..................	795							
LITTLE JEWEL								
Finger Lamp, Rare	650							
LITTLE MERMAID								
One Shape......................							90	
LITTLE OWL								
Hatpin, Rare......................	450*		1,100	1,200			800LV	
LITTLE STARS (MILLERSBURG)								
Bowl, 4", Rare...................			450					
Bowl, 7", Scarce.................	100	125	135	1,400			120CM	
Bowl, 9", Rare...................	450	550	575				400CM	
Bowl, 10½", Rare	600	700	750					
Plate, 7⅜", Rare			1,200					
LITTLE SWAN								
Miniature, 2"							75	
LOG								
Paperweight, 3" x 1¼", Rare....	150							
LOGANBERRY (IMPERIAL)								
Vase, Scarce	225	525	395				495AM	
Whimsey Vase		2,400						
LONG HOBSTAR								
Bowl, 8½"	45							
Bowl, 10½"	60							
Compote...........................	65							
Punch Bowl and Base..........	125						135CM	
LONG HORN								
Wine..............................	60							
LONG LEAF (DUGAN)								
Bowl, Ftd.............................					165			
LONG PRISMS								
Hatpin............................		75						
LONG THUMBPRINT (DUGAN)								
Vase, 7"-11"........................	30	35	40	40	150			
Bowl, 8¼"	30	40						
Compote...........................	35	40	40					
Creamer, Sugar, ea	40						50SM	
Butter	70							
LOTUS AND GRAPE (FENTON)								
Bon-bon	45	65	70	60			195AQ	950
Bowl, Flat, 7"......................	50	50	55	60				
Bowl, Ftd, 7".......................	55	60		70				
Plate, 9½", Rare	190	495	650	500				
LOTUS LAND (NORTHWOOD)								
Bon-bon	1,500							
LOUISA (WESTMORELAND)								
Rose Bowl.......................	55	65	70	67			150HO	
Candy Dish, Ftd	50	60	65				80AQ	
Bowl, Ftd..........................		50	50RG				70AQ	
Plate, Ftd, 8", Rare		155					190AG	
Mini-Banana Boat (old only) .	40	65						
LOVEBIRDS								
Bottle w/stopper..................	575							
LUCILE								
Pitcher, Rare......................	1,200			1,300				
Tumbler, Rare	750			800				
LUCKY BANK								
One Shape	40							
LUCKY BELL								
Bowl, 8¾", Rare	80							
LUSTER								
Tumbler	45							

Lustre Flute

Magpie

Many Stars

Maple Leaf

	M	A	G	B	PO	AO	Pas	R
LUSTRE AND CLEAR (FENTON)								
Fan Vase	40		60	55			90IG	
LUSTRE AND CLEAR (IMPERIAL)								
Pitcher...............................	195							
Creamer or Sugar	40	65					60	
Bowl, 5"..............................	20						30	
Bowl, 10"............................	40						50	
Shakers, pair......................	70							
Tumbler	40							
Butter Dish	75							
Console Set, 3 pcs.	60							165
LUSTRE AND CLEAR (LIGHTOLIER)								
Shade.................................	45							
LUSTRE FLUTE (NORTHWOOD)								
Bowl, 5½"	35							
Bowl, 8"..............................	40	55	54					
Bon-bon		60	60					
Creamer or Sugar	40	55	55					
Hat.....................................	30	40	40					
Compote..............................		50	45					
Sherbet	30							
Nappy..................................	40	45	40					
Punch Bowl and Base..........	150	165	150					
Cup	15	25	20					
LUSTRE ROSE (IMPERIAL)								
Bowl, Flat, 7"-11"	35	45	50				60CM	
Bowl, Ftd, 9"-12"	40	55	60				75	2,500
Fernery	50	60	65	45			275AM	
Plate, 6"-9"	58	70	75				140AM	
Butter	60	75	70				100AM	
Sugar	40	55	55				80AM	
Creamer or Spooner	40	55	55				70AM	
Berry Bowl, 8"-9"	40	40	48				40	
Berry Bowl, 5"	20	25	30				20	
Pitcher................................	85	100	110				100AM	
Rose Bowl...........................	60	70	80				70CL	
Tumbler	25	30	40				50AM	
Milk Pitcher........................	60						120AM	
Plate Whimsey, Ftd..............	50						65CM	
LUTZ (McKEE)								
Mug, Ftd	60							
MAGNOLIA DRAPE								
Pitcher................................	275							
Tumbler	55							
MAGPIE (AUSTRALIAN)								
Bowl, 6"-10"	45	60						
MAIZE (LIBBEY)								
Vase, Celery, Rare...............							185CL	
Syrup, Rare							235CL	
MAJESTIC (McKEE)								
Tumbler, Rare	500							
MALAGA (DUGAN)								
Bowl, 9" Scarce...................	60	80						
Plate, 10", Rare...................		350					375	
MANHATTAN (U.S. GLASS)								
Decanter	250*							
Wine...................................	40*							
MANY FRUITS (DUGAN)								
Punch Bowl w/base..............	450	900					1,400W	
Cup....................................	25	30	40	45			60W	
MANY PRISMS								
Perfume w/stopper..............	75							
MANY STARS (MILLERSBURG)								
Bowl, Ruffled, 9", Scarce......	350	575	475	2,000			1,850V	
Bowl, Round, 9½", Rare	500	1,000	700	2,100				
Tri-cornered Bowl, Rare.......		1,650						
MAPLE LEAF (DUGAN)								
Bowl, Stemmed, 9"	70	115		95				
Bowl, Stemmed, 4½"	30	35	50	30				
Butter	110	130		120				
Sugar	75	85		75				
Creamer or Spooner	50	65		60				
Pitcher................................	185	350		300				
Tumbler	30	50		40				

May Basket

Mikado

Mayan

Mayflower (Millersburg)

	M	A	G	B	PO	AO	Pas	R
MARIE (FENTON) Rustic Vase Interior Base Pattern								
MARILYN (MILLERSBURG)								
Pitcher, Rare	750	1,000	1,350					
Tumbler, Rare	150	275	400					
MARTEC (McKEE)								
Tumbler, Rare	500							
MARY ANN (DUGAN)								
Vase, 2 Varieties, 7"	75	135						
Loving Cup, 3 Handles, Rare	310*							
MASSACHUSETTS (U.S. GLASS)								
Vase	175*							
MAYAN (MILLERSBURG)								
Bowl, 8½"-10"	2,500*		200					
MAY BASKET (ENGLISH)								
Basket, 7½"			95					
Bowl, 9", Rare			160					
MAYFLOWER								
Bowl, 7½"	30	40			160		50	
Compote	40	50					60	
Shade	35							
Hat	40	50			150		60	
MAYFLOWER (MILLERSBURG) Exterior Pattern on Grape Leaves Bowls								
MAYPOLE								
Vase, 6¼"	45	55	60					
MELON RIB (IMPERIAL)								
Candy Jar w/lid	30							
Pitcher	60							
Tumbler	20							
Powder Jar w/lid	35							
Shakers, Pair	35							
Decanter	90							
MEMPHIS (NORTHWOOD)								
Bowl, 10"	100	195	200					
Bowl, 5"	35	45	50					
Fruit Bowl w/base	450	550	600	2,300			12,000IG	
Punch Bowl w/base	400	500	575				5,600IB	
Cup	30	40	45				75IB	
Sugar or Creamer		70						
MIKADO (FENTON)								
Compote, Large	250		2,400	700			650W	7,000*
MILADY (FENTON)								
Pitcher	500	700	800	975				
Tumbler	95	140	150	160				
MINIATURE BELL								
Paperweight, 2½"	60							
MINIATURE FLOWER BASKET (WESTMORELAND)								
One Shape	75							
MINIATURE HOBNAIL								
Cordial Set, Rare	1,250							
MINIATURE INTAGLIO (WESTMORELAND)								
Nut Cup, Stemmed, Rare	585						700W	
(Note: Also Known as "Wild Rose Wreath")								
MINIATURE SHELL								
Candleholder, Each							75CL	
MIRRORED PEACOCKS								
Tumbler, Rare	400							
MIRRORED LOTUS (FENTON)								
Bon-bon	85		100	95				
Bowl, 7"-8½"	60		90	80			900CeB	
Plate, 7½", Rare	400			550			3,000CeB	
Rose Bowl, Rare	375			480			1,100W	
MITERED DIAMOND AND PLEATS (ENGLISH)								
Bowl, 4½"	25			30				
Bowl, 8½", Shallow	40			45				
MITERED OVALS (MILLERSBURG)								
Vase, Rare	7,000	7,500	6,700					

	M	A	G	B	PO	AO	Pas	R
MOON AND STAR (WESTMORELAND)								
Compote (Pearl Carnival)							385	
MOONPRINT (ENGLISH)								
Bowl, 8¼"	45							
Candlesticks, Rare, Each.....	50							
Compote...........................	50							
Jar w/lid	60			85				
Vase	50							
Cheese Keeper, Rare	145							
Sugar, Stemmed	50							
Banana Boat, Rare	135							
Creamer	45							
Butter	100							
Bowl, 14"..........................	80							
Milk Pitcher, Scarce	150							
MORNING GLORY (IMPERIAL)								
Vase, 8"-16"......................	50+	90+	80+				80+SM	
Funeral Vase	185	200	220				180SM	
MORNING GLORY (MILLERSBURG)								
Pitcher, Rare......................	9,100	9,400	10,000					
Tumbler, Rare	1,100	1,400	1,000					
MOXIE								
Bottle, Rare							90	
MULTI-FRUITS AND FLOWERS (MILLERSBURG)								
Dessert, Stemmed, Rare		1,050	1,050					
Punch Bowl w/base, Rare	2,000	2,300	2,600	3,700				
Cup, Rare	50	75	90	175				
Pitcher, Rare (Either Base)......................	3,400	3,600	4,000*					
Tumbler, Rare	900	1,250	1,400					
MUSCADINE								
Tumbler, Rare	450							
MY LADY								
Powder Jar w/lid	90							
MYSTIC (CAMBRIDGE)								
Vase, Ftd, Rare	165							
NAPOLEON								
Bottle							85	
NARCISSUS AND RIBBON (FENTON)								
Wine Bottle w/stopper, Rare	1,150							
NAUTILUS (DUGAN-NORTHWOOD)								
Lettered, Rare.....................		285			250			
Unlettered		200			170			
Giant Compote, Rare	3,000*							
Vase Whimsey, Rare	1,750*	1,750*						
NEAR CUT (CAMBRIDGE)								
Decanter w/stopper, Rare			3,500					
NEAR CUT SOUVENIR (CAMBRIDGE)								
Mug, Rare	190							
Tumbler, Rare	260							
NEAR CUT WREATH (MILLERSBURG)								
Exterior Pattern Only								
NELL (HIGBEE)								
Mug..................................	75							
NESTING SWAN (MILLERSBURG)								
Rose Bowl, Rare	3,000							
Bowl, Scarce, Round or Ruffled, 10"	250	395	500	2,800*			2,650V*	
Spittoon Whimsey, Rare		5,000*	5,000*					
Bowl, Tri-Cornered, Rare	500	1,200	1,200	3,500			750CM	
NEW ORLEANS SHRINE (U.S. GLASS)								
Champagne..........................							150CL	
NIGHT STARS (MILLERSBURG)								
Bon-bon, Rare	500	450	400					
Card Tray, Rare...................		700						
Nappy, Tri-Cornered, Very Rare............................		1,000						
NIPPON (NORTHWOOD)								
Bowl, 8½"	250	220	325	350			450IG	
Plate, 9"............................	400	550	650	700			600W	

Moonprint

Morning Glory

My Lady's Powder Box

Near Cut Decanter

Nu-Art Chrysanthemum

Number 270

Octagon

Ohio Star

	M	A	G	B	PO	AO	Pas	R
NORRIS N. SMITH								
(NORTHWOOD)								
Advertising Plate, 5¾"		1,800						
NORTHERN STAR								
(FENTON)								
Card Tray, 6"	40							
Bowl, 6"-7"	30							
Plate, 6½", Rare	90							
NORTHWOOD								
JACK-IN THE PULPIT								
Vase, Various Sizes	40	50	45	50	90	225	85	
NORTHWOOD'S LOVELY								
Bowl, 9"								
(Leaf and Beads Exterior),								
Rare	600	600						
NORTHWOOD'S NEARCUT								
Compote	85	130						
Goblet, Rare	195	140						
Pitcher, Rare.......................	1,500*							
NORTHWOOD'S POPPY								
Bowl, 7"-8¾"	100	135		140	350*	595		
Pickle Dish, Oval	180	175	225	175		750	450IB	
Tray, Oval, Rare		300		375				
NU-ART								
(IMPERIAL)								
Plate, Scarce.......................	850	950	3,000	5,500			1,200W	
Shade................................	90							
NU-ART CHRYSANTHEMUM								
(IMPERIAL)								
Plate, Rare..........................	950	1,100	3,800	5,400			1,500AM*	
NUGGATE								
Pitcher 6"				90				
NUGGET BEADS								
Beads		125						
NUMBER 4								
(IMPERIAL)								
Bowl, Ftd............................	30						40SM	
Compote..............................	40							
NUMBER 270								
(WESTMORELAND)								
Compote..............................		90	140RG		115		140AQ	
NUMBER 2176 (SOWERBY)								
Lemon Squeezer	55							
NUMBER 2351								
(CAMBRIDGE)								
Bowl, 9", Rare......................			350*					
Punch Cup		65	65					
Punch Bowl/Base, Very Rare ..	1,500*							
NUMBER 600								
(FOSTORIA)								
Toothpick Holder	45							
OCTAGON								
(IMPERIAL)								
Bowl, 8½"	40		50				80	
Bowl, 4½"		35						
Goblet	65							
Butter	90		130					
Sugar	60		75					
Creamer or Spooner	55		65					
Toothpick Holder, Rare	70	85						
Pitcher...............................	120	400	240				200	
Tumbler	30	40	35				45	
Decanter, Complete	90	200	750					
Wine...................................	25	40	70					
Vase, Rare	90	140	125					
Milk Pitcher, Scarce	150	200	170				150	
Cordial							70	
Shakers, Pair, Old Only		160						
OCTET								
(NORTHWOOD)								
Bowl, 8½"	60	100					90W	
OHIO STAR								
(MILLERSBURG)								
Vase, Rare	1,300	1,500	1,400			13,000*	4,000W*	
Compote, Rare.....................	1,100							
Vase Whimsey, Rare		1,800*	1,800*			12,000*		
OKLAHOMA								
(MEXICAN)								
Tumble-Up, Complete..........	200							
Pitcher, Rare.......................	500*							
Tumbler, Rare	500							
Shade, Various Sizes,								
Rare							95CL	
OLYMPIC								
(MILLERSBURG)								
Compote, Small,								
Rare		3,500*	3,500*					

38

Open Rose

Optic and Buttons

Oriental Poppy

Ostrich Cake Plate

	M	A	G	B	PO	AO	Pas	R
OLYMPUS								
Shade	60							
OMNIBUS								
Tumbler, Rare	275		795	795				
OPEN FLOWER								
(DUGAN)								
Bowl, Flat or Ftd, 7"	35	45	50		85			
OPEN ROSE								
(IMPERIAL)								
Fruit Bowl, 7"-10"	40	65					70	
Bowl, Ftd, 9"-12"	65	45					95	
Bowl, Flat, 9"	45	40		50			65	
Bowl, Flat, 5½"	20	40					45	
Plate, 9"	65	180	185				185AM	
OPTIC								
(IMPERIAL)								
Bowl, 9"		75						
Bowl, 6"		50						
OPTIC AND BUTTONS								
(IMPERIAL)								
Bowls, 5"-8"	30							
Bowl, Handled, 12"	45							
Pitcher, Small, Rare	185							
Plate, 10½"	70							
Salt Cup	50							
Tumbler, 2 Shapes,								
Rare	110							
Goblet	60							
Cup and saucer, Rare	185							
OPTIC FLUTE								
(IMPERIAL)								
Bowl, 10"	45	80					55SM	
Bowl, 5"	30	45					30SM	
Compote	55							
OPTIC 66								
(FOSTORIA)								
Goblet	47							
ORANGE PEEL								
(WESTMORELAND)								
Punch Bowl w/base	200	225					225TL	
Cup	20	30					35TL	
Custard Cup, Scarce	25							
Dessert, Stemmed, Scarce	45	65	70RG				75TL	
ORANGE TREE								
(FENTON)								
Butter	250			350			340W	
Bowl, Flat, 8"-10"	55		235	95			500IM	1,400
Bowl, Ftd, 9"-11"	55		140	130			120W	
Ice Cream, w/stem, Small	30			35				
Bowl, Ftd, 5½"	40		45	48			900CeB	
Breakfast Set, 2 Pieces	180		230	220			250W	
Plate, 8"-9½"	235			450			400CM	
Powder Jar w/lid	75		500	95			130W	
Mug, 2 Sizes	70	80						
Loving Cup	160		350	275	4,500*	5,500*	500W	
Punch Bowl w/base	200		300	275	1,000MO*		400W	
Cup	30		36	32			38W	
Compote, Small	50	60	90	50				
Goblet, Large	90						85AQ	
Wine	25					75	70SM	
Sugar	65			75			150W	
Pitcher, 2 Designs	220			325			9,000LO*	
Tumbler	35			42			75W	
Creamer or Spooner	45			65			120W	
Rose Bowl	55	65	70	65			275W	1,900
Hatpin Holder	160		350	290			300W	
Hatpin Holder Whimsey,								
Rare				2,600				
Centerpiece Bowl, Rare	900		1,200	1,600				
Cruet Whimsey, Rare				1,250				
Orange Bowl Whimsey, 12"			650					
ORANGE TREE AND SCROLL								
(FENTON)								
Pitcher	495		600	550				
Tumbler	50		85	80				
ORANGE TREE ORCHARD								
(FENTON)								
Pitcher	400	500	550	500			650W	
Tumbler	40	50	55	50			120W	
ORIENTAL POPPY								
(NORTHWOOD)								
Pitcher	500	700	950	3,200			1,100W	
Tumbler	40	75	55	275			200W	
OSTRICH								
(AUSTRALIAN)								
Compote, Large, Rare	150	200						
Cake Stand, Rare	275	350						

Oval and Round

Palm Beach

Panelled Dandelion

Panelled Smocking

	M	A	G	B	PO	AO	Pas	R
OVAL AND ROUND (IMPERIAL)								
Plate, 10"	65	75	80				90AM	
Bowl, 4"	20	30	30					
Bowl, 7"	30	36	40				45AM	
Bowl, 9"	35	45	50				60AM	
OVAL PRISMS								
Hatpin		75						
OVAL STAR AND FAN (JENKINS)								
Rose Bowl	50	60						
OWL BANK								
One Size	40							
OWL BOTTLE								
One Shape							65CL	
OXFORD								
Mustard Pot w/lid	70							
PACIFICA (U.S. GLASS)								
Tumbler	400							
PAINTED CASTLE								
Shade	65							
PAINTED PANSY								
Fan Vase	50							
PALM BEACH (U.S. GLASS)								
Vase Whimsey	85	125					140W	
Bowl, 9"	55						75	
Bowl, 5"	30						50	
Butter	120						225	
Creamer, Spooner, Sugar, Each	75						125	
Pitcher	300						600W	
Tumbler	80						140W	
Plate, 9", Rare	175	250					225	
Banana Bowl	100	200						
Rose Bowl Whimsey, Rare	90						210W	
PANAMA (U.S. GLASS)								
Goblet, Rare	135							
PANELLED CRUET								
One Size	95							
PANELLED DANDELION (FENTON)								
Pitcher	400	425	550	575				
Tumbler	50	55	60	70				
Candle Lamp Whimsey, Rare				3,200				
Vase Whimsey, Rare				3,500*				
PANELLED DIAMOND AND BOWS (FENTON)								
Vase, 7"-14"	35	40	40	40	85		75	
Also called "Boggy Bayou"								
PANELLED HOBNAIL (DUGAN)								
Vase, 5"-10"	40	60	75		85		95	
PANELLED PALM (U.S. GLASS)								
Mug, Rare	95							
PANELLED PRISM								
Jam Jar w/lid	55							
PANELLED SMOCKING								
Sugar	50							
PANELLED SWIRL								
Rose Bowl	65							
PANELLED THISTLE (HIGBEE)								
Tumbler	100							
PANELLED TREE TRUNK (DUGAN)								
Vase, 7"-12", Rare	70	90	110		150			
PANELS AND BALL (FENTON)								
Bowl, 11"	60						175W	
Also Called "Persian Pearl"								
PANELS AND BEADS								
Shade							55VO	
PANSY (IMPERIAL)								
Bowl, 8¾"	40	95	85	110			80AQ	
Creamer or Sugar	25	40	45				50SM	
Dresser Tray	60	90	80				100SM	
Pickle Dish, Oval	30	50	40	95			60SM	
Nappy, Old Only	20		27					
Plate, Ruffled, Rare	80	195	120				100SM	

Parlor Panels

Peacock

Peacock and Grapes

Peacock Lamp

	M	A	G	B	PO	AO	Pas	R
PANTHER								
(FENTON)								
Bowl, Ftd, 10"	135	340	900	250		5,500NG	780W	
Bowl, Ftd, 5"	55		400				350W	1,450
Whimsey Bowl, 10½"	950			1,000				
PAPERWEIGHT								
Flower-Shaped,								
Rare							200	
PARLOR								
Ashtray				95				
PARLOR PANELS								
Vase, 4"-11"	50	190	250	200			450SM	
PASTEL HAT								
Various Sizes	50+						50+	
PASTEL PANELS								
(IMPERIAL)								
Pitcher							300	
Tumbler							75	
Mug, Stemmed							90	
Creamer or Sugar							65	
PEACH								
(NORTHWOOD)								
Bowl, 9"							150W	
Bowl, 5"							50W	
Butter							275W	
Creamer, Sugar, or								
Spooner, ea	275*						150W	
Pitcher				650			775W	
Tumbler				85EB			100W	
PEACH BLOSSOM								
Bowl, 7½"	60	75						
PEACH AND PEAR								
(DUGAN)								
Banana Bowl	70	95						
PEACHES								
Wine Bottle	45							
PEACOCK, FLUFFY								
(FENTON)								
Pitcher	500	600	700	800				
Tumbler	45	55	60	65				
PEACOCK								
(MILLERSBURG)								
Bowl, 9"	375	550	500				650CM	
Bowl, 5"	90	135	240	1,000				
Bowl, Vt, 7½"								
Rare	500	500	450					
Bowl, Vt, 6"								
Rare		150						
Ice Cream Bowl, 5"	60	90	140	390				
Plate, 6", Rare	900	800						
Spittoon Whimsey,								
Rare	5,600	7,000						
Proof Whimsey,								
Rare	300	270	300					
Rose Bowl Whimsey,								
Rare		4,600						
Bowl, 10", Ice Cream,								
Rare	500	700	1,000					
Banana Bowl, Rare		3,500						
PEACOCK AND DAHLIA								
(FENTON)								
Bowl, 7½"	50		125	100			150W	
Plate, 8½",								
Rare	390			450				
PEACOCK GARDEN								
(NORTHWOOD)								
Vase, 8", Rare	4,200						3,000*	
PEACOCK AND GRAPE								
(FENTON)								
Bow, Flat or Ftd, 7¾"	50	175	175	150	250		450V	795
Plate, 9" (Either Base),								
Rare	550	425		450			395	
PEACOCK LAMP								
Carnival Base	800	450	495				550W	750
PEACOCK, STRUTTING								
(WESTMORELAND)								
Creamer or Sugar								
w/lid		65	65					
PEACOCK TAIL								
(FENTON)								
Bon-bon	75	75	90	55				
Bowl, 4"-10"	40	50	60	55	650			1,800
Compote	35	45	60	50			55W	
Hat	30	40	55	50				
Hat, Advertising	40		50					
Plate, 9"	200	225		175				
Plate, 6"	70	80		70				

Peacock at the Fountain
(Northwood)

Peacock Tail

People's Vase

Perfection

	M	A	G	B	PO	AO	Pas	R
PEACOCK AND URN (FENTON)								
Bowl, 8½"	150	325	300	200				
Plate, 9"	650	500	900	800			550W	
Compote	55	70	90	75			125W	
Goblet, Rare	70	100		85			110W	
PEACOCK AND URN (NORTHWOOD)								
Bowl, 9"	200	475	650			500LV	500LV	
Bowl, Ice Cream, 10"	400	500	790	900		31,000	1,100IG	
Bowl, 5"	75	90	110					
Bowl, Ice Cream, 6"	350	160	185	125		2,700	250IG	
Plate, 11", Rare	2,100	1,200						
Plate, 6", Rare	450	550						
(Add 10% If Stippled)								
PEACOCK AND URN AND VTS. (MILLERSBURG)								
Bowl, 9½"	350	400	375	2,000*				
Compote, Large, Rare	1,350	1,500	1,350					
Bowl, Ice Cream, 10" Rare	500	700	2,600	2,000*				
Bowl, Ice Cream, 6" Rare	300	150	290	750				
Ruffled Bowl, 6"	190	145	210					
Plate, 10½", Rare	2,900							
Mystery Bowl, Variant, 8¾" Rare	350	450	390	1,350				
PEACOCK AT THE FOUNTAIN (DUGAN)								
Pitcher				600				
Tumbler		90		80				
PEACOCK AT THE FOUNTAIN (NORTHWOOD)								
Bowl, 9"	75	95	145	100			600IG	
Bowl, 5"	45	60	95	75			275W	
Orange Bowl, Ftd	450	650	3,500	900		10,000		
Punch Bowl w/base	450	550		600		30,000	5,200W	
Cup	30	45		55		1,400	125W	
Butter	265	345	400	325				
Sugar	200	300	370	250				
Creamer or Spooner	100	100	300	225				
Compote, Rare	375	450		500		3,800	1,400IG	
Pitcher	375	650	1,700	700			800W	
Tumbler	40	50	500	80			240W	
Spittoon Whimsey, Rare			4,200					
PEACOCK TAIL VT. (MILLERSBURG)								
Compote, Scarce	90	120	110					
PEACOCK TAIL AND DAISY								
Bowl, Very Rare	1,500	1,850*				2,200BO*		
PEACOCKS (ON FENCE) (NORTHWOOD)								
Bowl, 8¾"	300	450	600	450		3,300	1,000IG	
Plate, 9"	500	950	1,300	1,200EB		4,800	1,600IB	
PEARL AND JEWELS (FENTON)								
Basket, 4"							200W	
PEARL LADY (NORTHWOOD)								
Shade							90PG	
PEARL #37 (NORTHWOOD)								
Shade							100PO	
PEBBLE AND FAN (ENGLISH)								
Vase, 11¼", Rare				750*			750AM*	
PENNY								
Match Holder, Rare		250						
PEPPER PLANT (FENTON)								
Hat Shape				200				
PERFECTION (MILLERSBURG)								
Pitcher, Rare	4,000	4,000	4,500					
Tumbler, Rare	600	400	650					

Persian Garden

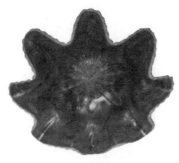

Petal and Fan

Petals

Peter Rabbit

	M	A	G	B	PO	AO	Pas	R
PERSIAN GARDEN (DUGAN)								
Bowl, Ice Cream, 11"	295	1,100	500	450	650		350W	
Bowl, Ice Cream, 6"	140	165	150	135	170		105W	
Bowl, Berry, 10"	190	220					300	
Bowl, Berry, 5"	50	60			80		100	
Plate, Chop, 13" Rare		11,000			4,800		2,200W	
Plate, 6", Rare	90	150					250W	
Fruit Bowl, w/base	110	420			500			
PERSIAN MEDALLION (FENTON)								
Bon-bon	35	55	60	50			200AQ	1,000
Compote	75	400	190	85			650W	
Bowl, 10"	75	210	300	550				
Bowl, 5"	48	55	40	60				1,100
Bowl, 8¾"	60	90						950
Orange Bowl	95	300	250	275				
Rose Bowl	60	70	80	70				
Plate, 7"	50	250		200			700V	
Plate, 9½"		450		425			500W	
Hair Receiver	70	90		80			110	
Punch Bowl/Base	265	400	500	375				
Punch Cup	25	35	40	30				
PETAL AND FAN (DUGAN)								
Bowl, 10"	275	525	400		340		300	
Bowl, 5"	35	60	50		40		60	
Bowl, 8½"	65	95						
Plate, Ruffled, 6"		750						
PETALS (DUGAN)								
Bowl, 8¾"	40	55			110		70	
Compote	47	60					85	
Banana Bowl		90			110			
PETER RABBIT (FENTON)								
Bowl, 9", Rare	1,100		1,250	1,200				
Plate, 10", Rare	1,700		2,200	1,700			1,800AM	
PICKLE								
Paperweight, 4½"		65						
PIGEON								
Paperweight	190							
PILLAR AND DRAPE								
Shade					70MO		90W	750
PILLAR AND FLUTE (IMPERIAL)								
Compote	50						55SM	
Rose Bowl	60						75SM	
Creamer or sugar	35						40SM	
Celery Vase	60	90					85SM	
PILLOW AND SUNBURST (WESTMORELAND)								
Bowl, 7½"-9"	45	60			70		65AM	
PINCHED RIBS								
Vase	85				180			
PINE CONE (FENTON)								
Bowl, 6"	125	250	350	200			250W	
Plate, 6½"	150	175	275	125				
Plate, 8", Rare			250	225				
PINEAPPLE (ENGLISH)								
Bowl, 7"	60	70		67				
Bowl, 4"	40							
Creamer	70	100						
Sugar, Stemmed or Flat	75							
Compote	50	70		58				
Butter	85							
Rose Bowl	55							
PINEAPPLE, HEAVY (FENTON)								
Bowl, Ftd, 10" Rare	750			950			900W	
PIN-UPS (AUSTRALIAN)								
Bowl, 8¾", Rare	110	140						
PINWHEEL (DUGAN)								
Bowl, 6"	50				85			
Plate, 6½"	2,000							
PINWHEEL (ENGLISH)								
Vase, 6½"	100	120						
Vase, 8"	120	140						
Bowl, 8", Rare	50							
(Also Called Derby)								

Poinsettia (Imperial)

Plain Jane Basket

Pony

Pretty Panels

	M	A	G	B	PO	AO	Pas	R
PIPE HUMIDOR (MILLERSBURG)								
Tobacco Jar w/lid, Rare.......	5,000	7,000	6,500					
PLAID (FENTON)								
Bowl, 8¾"	120HA		350	200			950CeB	5,000
Plate, 9", Rare.....................	350			450				7,900
PLAIN JANE								
Paperweight.........................	90							
PLAIN JANE (IMPERIAL)								
Basket.................................	60						75SM	
PLAIN PETALS (NORTHWOOD)								
Nappy, Scarce		85	90					
(Interior of Leaf and Beads Nappy)								
PLEATS AND HEARTS								
Shade.................................							90	
PLUMS AND CHERRIES (NORTHWOOD)								
Sugar, Rare				1,750				
Spooner, Rare.....................				1,750				
Tumbler				4,000*				
PLUME PANELS								
Vase, 7"-12"........................	50	70	80	65			150	850
POINSETTIA (IMPERIAL)								
Milk Pitcher........................	170	950	275				450SM	
POINSETTIA (NORTHWOOD)								
Bowl, Flat or Ftd, 8½"	400	575	750	1,000EB		4,000	3,500IB	
(Also Called Poinsettia & Lattice)								
POLO								
Ashtray	85							
POND LILY (FENTON)								
Bon-bon	45		65	60			75W	
PONY (DUGAN)								
Bowl, 8½"	120	260					1,100IG	
Plate, Age Questionable, 9", Rare, ...	450*							
POODLE								
Powder Jar w/lid	30							
POOL OF PEARLS								
Exterior pattern only								
POPPY (MILLERSBURG)								
Compote, Scarce..................	650	695	500					
Salver, Rare	1,200	1,450	1,600					
POPPY AND FISH NET (IMPERIAL)								
Vase, 6", Rare								750
POPPY SHOW (IMPERIAL)								
Vase, 12", Old Only..............	450	1,700	950				1,000SM	
Hurricane Whimsey		2,500					2,500W	
Lamp Whimsey....................	2,500*							
POPPY SHOW (NORTHWOOD)								
Bowl, 8½"	750	600	900	1,700			1,700IG	
Plate, 9", Rare....................	1,700	1,400	3,000	5,500EB			700W	
POPPY WREATH (NORTHWOOD)								
(Amaryllis Exterior Pattern)								
PORTLAND (U.S. GLASS)								
Bowl, 8½"							170	
POTPOURRI (MILLERSBURG)								
Milk Pitcher, Rare................	2,000*							
PRAYER RUG (FENTON)								
Bon-bon, Rare					1,800IC			
(Iridized Custard Only)								
PREMIUM (IMPERIAL)								
Candlesticks, Pair................	60	90					80	150
Bowl, 8½"	45	80					80	110
Bowl, 12".............................	55	75					90	130
Under Plate, 14"	50	90					120	150
PRETTY PANELS (FENTON)								
Pitcher w/lid								500
Tumbler, Handled...............	60							90IG

44

Primrose

Primrose and Fishnet

Prism and Daisy Band

Queen's Lamp

	M	A	G	B	PO	AO	Pas	R
PRETTY PANELS (NORTHWOOD)								
Pitcher..................	125		150					
Tumbler	60		70					
PRIMROSE (MILLERSBURG)								
Bowl, Ruffled, 8¾"...........	90	185	175	3,000			160CM	
Bowl, Ice Cream, 9", Scarce .	110	190	190					
Bowl, Experimental, Goofus Exterior, Rare		900						
PRIMROSE AND FISHNET (IMPERIAL)								
Vase, 6", Rare								750
PRIMROSE PANELS (IMPERIAL)								
Shade..............................							60	
PRIMROSE RIBBON								
Lightshade	90							
PRINCELY PLUMES								
Candle Holder		300						
PRINCESS (U.S. GLASS)								
Lamp, Complete, Rare		1,800						
PRISM								
Shakers, Pair......................	60							
Tray, 3"	50							
Hatpin.............................		75						
PRISM BAND (FENTON)								
Pitcher, Decorated	175	350	395	410			350W	
Tumbler, Decorated	30	50	55	55			150W	
PRISM AND CANE (ENGLISH)								
Bowl, 5", Rare.....................	45	65						
PRISM AND DAISY BAND (IMPERIAL)								
Vase	28							
Compote...........................	35							
Bowl, 5"............................	18							
Bowl, 8"............................	30							
Sugar or Creamer, Each	35							
PRISMS (WESTMORELAND)								
Compote, 5", Scarce	50	90	100				150TL	
PROPELLER (IMPERIAL)								
Bowl, 9½", Rare	80							
Compote...........................	35		45				55SM	
Vase, Stemmed, Rare...........	90							
PROUD PUSS (CAMBRIDGE)								
Bottle	85							
PULLED LOOP (DUGAN)								
Vase	40	60	50	110			650CeB	
PUMP, HOBNAIL (NORTHWOOD)								
One Shape, Age Questionable			850					
PUMP, TOWN (NORTHWOOD)								
One Shape, Rare	1,100	790	1,350					
PUZZLE (DUGAN)								
Compote............................	40	50	75	85	90		75W	
Bon-bon, Stemmed..............	40	50	90	125	100		80W	
PUZZLE PIECE								
One Shape.........................				100*				
QUARTERED BLOCK								
Creamer	60							
Sugar	60							
Butter	125							
QUEEN'S JEWEL								
Goblet	55							
QUEEN'S LAMP								
One Shape, Rare			2,500					
QUESTION MARKS (DUGAN)								
Bon-bon	40	55			60		80IG	
Compote...........................	40	70			75		70W	
Cake Plate, Stemmed, Rare..		450*						
QUILL (DUGAN)								
Pitcher, Rare......................	2,000	3,500						
Tumbler, Rare	400	500						
RADIANCE								
Pitcher.............................	240							
Tumbler	90							

	M	A	G	B	PO	AO	Pas	R
RAGGED ROBIN (FENTON)								
Bowl, 8¾", Scarce	75	100	100	100			150W	
RAINBOW (NORTHWOOD)								
Bowl, 8"..............................		80	95					
Compote.............................		110	150					
Plate, 9"..............................		135	160					
RAINDROPS (DUGAN)								
Bowl, 9"..............................	65	80			100			
Banana Bowl, 9¾"		150			165			
RAMBLER ROSE (DUGAN)								
Pitcher................................	160	250	275	220				
Tumbler	30	50	55	45				
RANGER (MEXICAN)								
Creamer	40							
Nappy..................................	90							
Tumbler	290							
Milk Pitcher........................	175							
Sugar	150							
Butter	190							
Breakfast Set, 2 Pieces	175							
Perfume, 5¼"	150*							
Pitcher, Rare......................	295							
Shot Glass, Rare.................	425							
RANGER TOOTHPICK								
Toothpick Holder	95							
Vase, 10"............................	50						65SM	
RASPBERRY (NORTHWOOD)								
Bowl, 9"..............................	60	70	75					
Bowl, 5"..............................	30	35	40					
Milk Pitcher........................	150	225	275				2,000IB	
Sauce Boat, Ftd...................	90	150	275	190			350TL	
Pitcher................................	165	275	295				2,200IB	
Tumbler	45	45	60				200IB	
Compote..............................	48	56	58					
RAYS (DUGAN)								
Bowl, 5"..............................	40	50	50	75				
Bowl, 9"..............................	55	90	90	125				
RAYS AND RIBBONS (MILLERSBURG)								
Bowl, Round or Ruffled, 8½"-9½"	65	90	90				300V	
Plate, Rare..........................	1,100							
Banana Bowl, Rare..............			1,000					
Bowl, Tri-Cornered or Square	115	140	150					
RED PANELS (IMPERIAL)								
Shade..................................								200
REGAL IRIS (CONSOLIDATED GLASS)								
"Gone With The Wind" Lamp, Rare	3,700							12,000*
REGAL SWIRL								
Candlestick, Each................	75							
REX								
Pitcher................................	375							
Tumbler	60							
RIB AND PANEL (FENTON)								
Vase	50	60		65		125		
Spittoon Whimsey................	250							
RIBBED ELIPSE (HIGBEE)								
Mug, Rare							150HA	
RIBBED HOLLY (FENTON)								
Compote..............................	50	70		60				350
Goblet	75	100		85				390
RIBBED SWIRL								
Tumbler	60		80					
Bowl, 9"..............................	55		75					
RIBBON AND BLOCK								
Lamp, Complete	600							
RIBBON AND FERN								
Atomizer, 7"........................	90							
RIBBON AND LEAVES								
Sugar, Small........................	50							
RIBBON TIE (FENTON)								
Bowl, 8¾"	50	60	75	135				5,600
Plate, Ruffled, 9".................				175				7,500*
Plate, Flat, 9½"				360				

Ragged Robin

Raspberry

Rays

Ribbon Tie

Robin

Roman Rosette

Rosalind

Rose and Greek Key

	M	A	G	B	PO	AO	Pas	R
RIBS (CZECHOSLOVAKIA)								
Ringtree	60							
Puff Box	95							
Pinbox................................	75							
Perfume or Cologne	110							
Soap Dish............................	60							
Dresser Tray........................	110							
RINGS (JEANETTE)								
Vase, 8"	55							
RIPPLE (IMPERIAL)								
Vase, Various Sizes..............	60	150	190	110			350TL	
RISING SUN (U.S. GLASS)								
Butterdish...........................	175							
Creamer	90							
Sugar	125							
Pitcher, 2 Shapes, Rare........	1,000*		2,000*					
Tumbler, Rare	400			600				
Tray, Rare				500				
Juice Tumbler, Rare	1,000							
ROBIN (IMPERIAL)								
Mug, Old Only	55						160	
Pitcher, Old Only, Scarce.....	300							
Tumbler, Old Only, Scarce...	60							
ROCK CRYSTAL (McKEE)								
Punch Bowl w/base.............		600						
Cup.....................................		45						
ROCOCO (IMPERIAL)								
Bowl, 5"...............................	40		150				90SM	
Vase, 5½"............................	95		175				150SM	
ROLL								
Tumbler	40							
Cordial Set, Complete	350							
(Decanter, Stopper, 6 Glasses)								
Pitcher, Rare.......................							300CL	
Shakers, Rare, Each............	45							
ROLLED RIBS								
Bowl (Marigold Opal)							150	
ROMAN ROSETTE (U.S. GLASS)								
Goblet, 6", Rare							110CL	
ROOD'S CHOCOLATES (FENTON)								
Advertising Plate.................		2,000*						
ROSALIND (MILLERSBURG)								
Bowl, 10" Scarce..................	175	260	325				500AQ	
Bowl, 5", Rare.....................	200	295	575					
Compote, 6", Rare (Variant)		550	500					
Compote, Ruffled, 8", Rare	1,000							
Compote, Jelly, 9", Rare	1,800	2,000	2,000					
Plate, 9" Very Rare..............	2,500							
ROSE								
Bottle							130	
ROSE BAND								
Tumbler, Rare	700							
ROSE BOUQUET								
Creamer	60							
Bon-bon, Rare	75						400W	
ROSE COLUMN (MILLERSBURG)								
Vase, Rare	1,800	1,600	1,200	8,000				
Experimental Vase, Rare......		4,600						
ROSE GARDEN (SWEDEN)								
Letter Vase	180			190				
Bowl, 8¾"	80	80		75				
Vase, Round, 9"	385			250				
Pitcher, Communion, Rare	1,300			1,600				
Bowl, 6", Rare......................		90						
Butter, Rare.........................	450			445				
Rose Bowl, Small, Rare........	900							
Rose Bowl, Large, Rare				700				
ROSE AND GREEK KEY								
Square Plate, Rare							8,000AM*	
ROSE PANELS (AUSTRALIAN)								
Compote, Large	145							

Royalty

Rosette

Rose Tree

Rose Spray Compote

	M	A	G	B	PO	AO	Pas	R
ROSE PINWHEEL								
Bowl, Rare	1,900		2,200					
ROSE SHOW (NORTHWOOD)								
Bowl, 8¾"	500	600	3,000	800EB		2,400	1,900IB	
Plate	1,900	2,300	8,000	1,100	12,000MC	6,000	750W	
ROSE SHOW VARIANT (NORTHWOOD)								
Plate, 9"	1,800	1,900	2,200	3,800RenB	3,000		2,500IB	
Bowl, 8¾"	700	750		900			700W	
ROSE SPRAY (FENTON)								
Compote	175						190	
ROSE TREE (FENTON)								
Bowl, 10", Rare	1,150			1,200				
ROSE WINDOWS								
Tumbler, Rare	400							
ROSE WREATH (Basket of Roses) (NORTHWOOD)								
Bon-bon, Rare	275	350		350				
(Basketweave Exterior)								
ROSES AND FRUIT (MILLERSBURG)								
Bon-bon, Ftd, Rare	1,200	1,800	2,000	3,000				
ROSES AND RUFFLES (CONSOLIDATED GLASS)								
G-W-T-W Lamp, Rare	2,900							10,000
ROSETIME								
Vase	100							
ROSETTES (NORTHWOOD)								
Bowl, Dome Base, 9"	50	75						
Bowl, Ftd, 7"		80						
ROUND-UP (DUGAN)								
Bowl, 8¾"	100	180		140	175		180W	
Plate, 9", Rare	185	225		170	225		325W	
ROYALTY (IMPERIAL)								
Punch Bowl w/base	140							
Cup	30							
Fruit Bowl w/stand	100						140SM	
RUFFLED RIB (NORTHWOOD)								
Spittoon Whimsey, Rare	225							
Bowl, 8"-10"	50	70						
Vase, 7"-14"	70							
RUFFLES AND RINGS (NORTHWOOD)								
Exterior Pattern Only								
RUFFLES, RINGS AND DAISY BAND (NORTHWOOD)								
Bowl, Ftd, Rare, 8½"					1,000MO			
RUSTIC (FENTON)								
Vase, Funeral, 15"-20"	120	150	220	175				
Vase, Various Sizes	40	50	60	55	75		80	3,700
S-BAND (AUSTRALIAN)								
Compote	70	95						
S-REPEAT (DUGAN)								
Creamer, Small		75						
Punch Bowl w/base, Rare		1,800						
Cup, Rare		120						
Toothpick Holder (Old Only), Rare		85						
Tumbler	300							
Sugar, Rare (Very Light Iridescence)		250						
SACIC (ENGLISH)								
Ashtray	70							
SAILBOATS (FENTON)								
Bowl, 6"	38		75	70			125AM	550
Goblet	250	380	275	70			190	
Wine	35			100				
Compote	65			150				
Plate	470			400			350AM	
SAILING SHIP								
Plate, 8"	40							

	M	A	G	B	PO	AO	Pas	R
SAINT (ENGLISH)								
Candlestick, Each................	300							
SALAMANDERS								
Hatpin..................................		75						
SALT CUP (VARIOUS MAKERS)								
One Shape, Averaged...........	45	55	88RG				75CeB	
SATIN SWIRL								
Atomizer..............................							75CL	
SAWTOOTH BAND								
Tumbler Rare	400							
SAWTOOTH PRISMS								
Jelly Jar	60							
SCALE BAND (FENTON)								
Bowl, 6"...............................	35				80			
Plate, Flat, 6½"	45						85V	585
Plate, Dome Base, 7"	50							550
Pitcher.................................	125			400				
Tumbler	60			350				
SCALES (WESTMORELAND)								
Bon-bon	40	48			90	300	60TL	
Bowl, 7"-10"					90IM		46TL	
Deep Bowl, 5"		40						
Plate, 6"..............................	45	58					65TL	
Plate, 9"..............................		95			110	260	140	
SCARAB								
Hatpin..................................		100					150AM	
SCOTCH THISTLE (FENTON)								
Compote...............................	46	60	75	50				
SCOTTIE								
Powder Jar w/lid	35							
Paperweight, Rare................	250							
SCROLL (WESTMORELAND)								
Pin Tray	50							
SCROLL AND FLOWER PANELS (IMPERIAL)								
Vase, 10", Old Only..............	95	250		150				
SCROLL EMBOSSED (IMPERIAL)								
Bowl, 8½"	40	65						600
Dessert, Round or Ruffled, Rare	90	275	150					
Plate, 9"..............................		325	200				90TL	
Compote, Large	50	450					100AQ	
Compote, Small	40	75	60					
Sauce	35	55						
SCROLL EMBOSSED VT. (ENGLISH)								
Handled Ashtray, 5"	45	60						
Plate, 7"..............................	165							
SEACOAST (MILLERSBURG)								
Pin Tray, Rare	500	550	425				900CM	
SEAFOAM (DUGAN)								
Exterior Pattern Only								
SEAGULL (CZECH)								
Vase, Rare	1,150							
SEAGULLS (DUGAN)								
Bowl, 6½", Scarce	80							
SEAWEED								
Lamp, 2 Sizes	250							
Lamp Vt., 8½", Rare.............							395IB	
SEAWEED (MILLERSBURG)								
Bowl, 5", Rare......................	400		470					
Bowl, 9", Rare......................	275		375	1,600			400CM	
Plate, 10", Rare....................	1,000	1,100	1,000					
Bowl, 10½", Ruffled, Scarce	350	400	350				300CM	
Bowl, Ice Cream, 10½", Rare....................................	400	450	500					
SERRATED RIBS								
Shaker, Each.......................	60							
SHARP								
Shot Glass...........................	50						70SM	
SHELL								
Shade..................................							75	
SHELL (IMPERIAL)								
Bowl, 7"-9"	45	250	75				90SM	
Plate, 8½"	190	1,050	375					
SHELL AND BALLS								
Perfume, 2½"	65							

Scale Band

Scottie

Scroll Embossed Variant

Sea Gulls Vase

Singing Birds

Single Flower Framed

Six Petals

Small Rib

	M	A	G	B	PO	AO	Pas	R
SHELL AND JEWEL (WESTMORELAND)								
Creamer w/lid	55	65	60				90W	
Sugar w/lid	55	65	60				90W	
SHERATON (U.S. GLASS)								
Pitcher							170	
Tumbler							50	
Butter							130	
Sugar							90	
Creamer or Spooner							75	
SHIP AND STARS								
Plate, 8"	40							
SHRINE (U.S. GLASS)								
Champagne							180CL	
Toothpick Holder		650					200CL	
SIGNET (ENGLISH)								
Sugar w/lid, 6½"	75							
SILVER AND GOLD								
Pitcher	150							
Tumbler	50							
SILVER QUEEN (FENTON)								
Pitcher	200							
Tumbler	70							
SINGING BIRDS (NORTHWOOD)								
Bowl, 10"	60	75	85					
Bowl, 5	30	35	40					
Mug	225	250	325	290		1,800	750W	
Butter	185	300	325					
Sugar	110	140	150					
Creamer	80	100	125					
Spooner	80	100	125					
Pitcher	350	375	550					
Tumbler	45	75	150					
Sherbet, Rare	300							
SINGLE FLOWER (DUGAN)								
Bowl, 8"	35	40	45		55			
Hat	30	40	40					
Handled Basket Whimsey, Rare	225				900			
Banana Bowl, 9½", Rare					350			
SINGLE FLOWER FRAMED (DUGAN)								
Bowl, 8¾"	65	90	80		130			
Bowl, 5"	40	50			75			
Plate		275			250			
SIX PETALS (DUGAN)								
Bowl, 8½"	40	125	70	80	75		60	
Plate, Rare	90	200	150		195			
Hat	45	50	60		80		150BA	
SIX-SIDED (IMPERIAL)								
Candlestick, Each	165	300	250				200SM	
SKATER'S SHOE (U.S. GLASS)								
One Shape	120							
SKI-STAR (DUGAN)								
Bowl, 8"-10"	60	95		175	150			
Bowl, 5"	40	50	60	55	80			
Basket, Handled, Rare					500			
Banana Bowl		125			290			
Plate, 7½"					160			
Hand Grip Bowl, 8"-10"					140			
Rose Bowl, Rare					600			
SMALL BASKET								
One Shape	50							
SMALL BLACKBERRY (NORTHWOOD)								
Compote	50	60	60					
SMALL PALMS								
Shade	45							
SMALL RIB (DUGAN)								
Compote	40	45	45				55AM	
Rose Bowl, Stemmed	40	45	50				55AM	
SMALL THUMBPRINT								
Creamer	60							
Toothpick Holder	70							

	M	A	G	B	PO	AO	Pas	R
SMITH REAL ESTATE								
Bowl	1,400							
SMOOTH PANELS (IMPERIAL)								
Bowl, 6½"	30						35PM	
Plate, 9¼"							90CL	
Tumbler							45PM	
Vase	40						250SMG	250
Pitcher	90		175					
SMOOTH RAYS (NORTHWOOD)								
Bon-bon	30						25CL	
SMOOTH RAYS (NORTHWOOD-DUGAN)								
Compote	40	50	55					
Rose Bowl	50	60			60			
Bowl, 6"-9"	45	90			80			
Plate, 7"-9"	60							
SMOOTH RAYS (WESTMORELAND)								
Compote			75				70AM	
Bowl, 7"-9", Flat	40	55	50		75		125BO	
Bowl, Dome Base, 5"-7½"			55		75		80TL	
SNOW FANCY (McKEE)								
Bowl, 5"			50					
Creamer or Sugar	50							
SODA GOLD (IMPERIAL)								
Candlestick, 3½", Each	55						60SM	
Bowl, 9"	45						60SM	
Pitcher	240						325SM	
Tumbler	40						75SM	
SODA GOLD SPEARS (DUGAN)								
Bowl, 8½"	40						40CL	
Bowl, 4½"	30						30CL	
Plate, 9"	50						160CL	
SOLDIERS AND SAILORS (FENTON)								
Plate (Illinois), Rare	1,000	1,600	1,750					
Plate (Indianapolis), Rare			3,500					
SOUTACHE (DUGAN)								
Bowl, 10"					200			
Plate, 10½", Rare					375			
Lamp, Complete	350							
SOUTHERN IVY								
Wine, 2 Sizes	45							
SOUVENIR BANDED								
Mug	85							
SOUVENIR BELL (IMPERIAL)								
One Shape, Lettering	180							
SOUVENIR MINIATURE								
One Shape, Lettering	50							
SOUVENIR MUG (McKEE)								
Any Lettering	65							
SOUVENIR PIN TRAY (U.S. GLASS)								
One Size							75	
(Same as Portland Pattern)								
SOUVENIR VASE (U.S. GLASS)								
Vase, 6½", Rare	100	135			150	400		
SOWERBY FLOWER BLOCK (ENGLISH)								
Flower Frog	60							
SOWERBY WIDE PANEL (SOWERBY)								
Bowl	45							
SPHINX (ENGLISH)								
Paperweight, Rare							595AM	
SPIDERWEB (NORTHWOOD)								
Candy Dish, covered							40SM	
SPIDERWEB (NORTHWOOD-DUGAN)								
Vase, 8"	50						80	
SPIDERWEB AND TREEBARK (DUGAN)								
Vase, 6"							65	
SPIRAL (IMPERIAL)								
Candlestick, Pair.	165	185	195				170SM	

Soda Gold

Soldiers and Sailors (Ill.)

Soutache

Stag and Holly

Star of David

Star of David and Bows

Star and Fan Cordial Set

	M	A	G	B	PO	AO	Pas	R
SPIRALEX (ENGLISH)								
Vase, Various Sizes	50	65	70	60			80	
SPIRALLED DIAMOND POINT								
Vase, 6"	90							
SPLIT DIAMOND (ENGLISH)								
Creamer, Small	40							
Sugar, Open	40							
Butter, Scarce	65							
SPOKES (FOSTORIA)								
Bowl, 10"							100	
SPRING BASKET (IMPERIAL)								
Handled Basket, 5"	50						65SM	
SPRING OPENING (MILLERSBURG)								
Plate, 6½", Rare		1,600						
SPRINGTIME (NORTHWOOD)								
Bowl, 9"	80	200	250					
Bowl, 5"	40	55	75					
Butter	375	450	475					
Sugar	300	400	425					
Creamer or Spooner	275	350	400					
Pitcher, Rare	750	1,000	1,250				1,800	
Tumbler, Rare	75	120	200				300	
STERLING FURNITURE (NORTHWOOD)								
Bowl		700						
STRETCHED DIAMONDS & DOTS								
Tumbler	175							
SQUARE DAISY AND BUTTON (IMPERIAL)								
Toothpick Holder, Rare							125	
SQUARE DIAMOND								
Vase, Rare				750				
STAG AND HOLLY (FENTON)								
Bowl, Ftd, 9"-13"	150	300	400	425	1,700		790AQ	3,000
Rose Bowl, Ftd	350		800	1,000				
Plate, Ftd, 13"	1,000							
Plate, Ftd, 9"	700	1,000		1,800				
STANDARD								
Vase, 5½"	50							
STAR								
Paperweight, Rare							295	
STAR (ENGLISH)								
Bowl, 8"	50							
STAR CENTER (IMPERIAL)								
Bowl, 8½"	30	40					50	
Plate, 9"	60	80					90	
STAR OF DAVID (IMPERIAL)								
Bowl, 8¾", Scarce	70	100	200				100SM	3,000*
STAR OF DAVID AND BOWS (NORTHWOOD)								
Bowl, 8½"	50	60	75				150AM	
STAR AND DIAMOND POINT								
Hatpin		75						
STAR AND FAN								
Vase, 9½", Rare	250			200				
(Note: Same as curved Star Pattern)								
STAR AND FAN (ENGLISH)								
Cordial Set	1,500							
(Decanter, 4 Stemmed Cordials and Tray)								
STAR AND FILE (IMPERIAL)								
Bowl, 7"-9½"	35							
Vase, Handled	50							
Compote	45							
Creamer or Sugar	30							
Pitcher	185							
Decanter w/stopper	110							
Rose Bowl	75	100	115				100AM	
Wine	75						250IG	
Spooner	30							
Sherbet	35							
Custard Cup	30							
Plate, 6"	65							
Pickle Dish	40							
Tumbler, Rare	275							
Bon-bon	35							

Starflower

Stippled Rays (Fenton)

Stippled Rays (Imperial)

Stippled Rays (Northwood)

	M	A	G	B	PO	AO	Pas	R
STAR AND HOBS								
Rose Bowl, 9", Rare				350				
STAR MEDALLION (IMPERIAL)								
Bon-bon	45							
Bowl, 7"-9"	30						40	
Compote	45							
Butter	100							
Creamer, Spooner or Sugar Each	60							
Milk Pitcher	80		95					
Goblet	45						60	
Tumbler	30		50				55	
Plate, 5"	60						45	
Plate, 10"							50	
Handled Celery	80						65	
Celery Tray	60						50	
Ice Cream, Stemmed, Small	35							
Pickle Dish	40							
Vase, 6"	40						45	
Custard Cup	20							
STAR AND NEARCUT								
Hatpin		60						
STAR AND ROSETTE								
Hatpin		75						
STAR SPRAY (IMPERIAL)								
Bowl, 7"	35						45SM	
Bride's Basket, Complete, Rare	90						125SM	
Plate, 7½", Scarce	75						95SM	
STARBRIGHT								
Vase, 6½"	40	45		50				
STARBURST								
Perfume w/stopper	65							
Spittoon	650							
STARFISH (DUGAN)								
Bon-bon, Handled, Rare		65			150		850	
Compote	40	65	75		125			
STARFLOWER								
Pitcher, Rare	3,200			2,750				
STARLYTE (IMPERIAL)								
Shade	40							
STARS AND BARS (CAMBRIDGE)								
Wine, Rare	150*							
STARS AND STRIPES (OLD GLORY)								
Plate, 7½", Rare	150*							
STIPPLED ACORNS								
Candy dish w/lid, Ftd	75	95		80				
STIPPLED DIAMOND SWAG (ENGLISH)								
Compote	45		65	60				
STIPPLED FLOWER (DUGAN)								
Bowl, 8½"					85			
STIPPLED PETALS (DUGAN)								
Bowl, 9"		75			90			
Handled Basket		150			165			
STIPPLED RAMBLER ROSE (DUGAN)								
Nut Bowl, Ftd	75			90				
STIPPLED RAYS (FENTON)								
Bon-bon	35	45	55	40				425
Bowl, 5"-9"	40	50	60	50				450
Compote	35	45	50	45				
Creamer or Sugar, Each	30	40	45	45				425
Plate, 7"	50	50	100	45				560
STIPPLED RAYS (IMPERIAL)								
Creamer, Stemmed	40		50				55SM	500
Sugar, Stemmed	40		50				55SM	500
Sugar Whimsey, Rare								600
STIPPLED RAYS (NORTHWOOD)								
Bowl, 8"-10"	45	55	65					
Compote	50	60	65					
STIPPLED SALT CUP								
One Size	45							

Stork ABC Plate

Stork and Rushes

Strawberry (Fenton)

Strawberry (Millersburg

	M	A	G	B	PO	AO	Pas	R
STIPPLED STRAWBERRY (JENKINS)								
Tumbler	60							
Creamer or Sugar	35							
Spittoon Whimsey, Rare	225							
Syrup, Rare	250							
Butter	85							
Bowl, 9", Rare	90	200						
STORK (JENKINS)								
Vase	60							
STORK ABC								
Child's Plate, 7½"	60							
STORK AND RUSHES (DUGAN)								
Butter, Rare	145	165						
Creamer or Spooner, Rare	80	90						
Sugar, Rare	90	120						
Bowl, 10"	40	50						
Bowl, 5"	30	30						
Mug	35	50		350				
Punch Bowl w/base, Rare	190	300		325				
Cup	20	30		35				
Hat	25			30				
Handled Basket	60							
Pitcher	250			400				
Tumbler	30	60		75				
STRAWBERRY (DUGAN)								
Epergne, Rare	1,000	900						
STRAWBERRY (FENTON)								
Bon-bon	55	50	65	60			90V	450
STRAWBERRY (MILLERSBURG)								
Bowl, 6½"	90	150	140					
Bowl, 8"-10", Scarce	285	450	400				1,300V	
Compote, Rare	575	300	325				1,950V	
Gravy Boat Whimsey, Rare							1,500V	
Banana Boat Whimsey, Rare		2,000*	2,000*				2,000V	
Bowl, 9½", Tri-Cornered	390	500	450					
STRAWBERRY (NORTHWOOD)								
Bowl, 8"-10"	75	90	85	90		2,200	1,100IG	
Bowl, 5"	45	60	70	80				
Plate, 9"	175	450	395	375		2,600		
Plate, Handgrip, 7"	190	250	275	230				
Stippled Plate, 9"	1,600	1,350	1,500					
STRAWBERRY INTAGLIO (NORTHWOOD)								
Bowl, 9½"	65							
Bowl, 5½"	30							
STRAWBERRY POINT								
Tumbler	150							
STRAWBERRY SCROLL (FENTON)								
Pitcher, Rare	1,900			2,500				
Tumbler, Rare	175			250				
STRAWBERRY SPRAY								
Brooch				175				
STRETCHED DIAMOND (NORTHWOOD)								
Tumbler, Rare	175							
STREAM OF HEARTS (FENTON)								
Bowl, Ftd, 10"	80			110				
Compote, Rare	95						135	
Goblet, Rare	200							
STRING OF BEADS								
One Shape	35		40					
STUDS (IMPERIAL)								
Tray, Large	65							
Juice, Tumbler	40							
Milk Pitcher	75							
STYLE								
Bowl, 8"		95						
SUMMER DAYS (DUGAN)								
Vase, 6"	60			70				
(Note: This is actually the base for the Stork and Rushes punch set.)								
SUN PUNCH								
Bottle	30						35	
SUNFLOWER (MILLERSBURG)								
Pin Tray, Rare	450	395	350					

Sun-Gold

Swan Pastel

Sunken Hollyhocks

	M	A	G	B	PO	AO	Pas	R
SUNFLOWER (NORTHWOOD)								
Bowl, 8½"	50	70	65	1,195ReB			1,900IB	
Plate, Rare	250		400					
SUNFLOWER AND DIAMOND								
Vase, 2 Sizes	75			110				
SUNGOLD (AUSTRALIAN)								
Epergne							450	
SUNK DIAMOND BAND (U.S. GLASS)								
Pitcher, Rare	150						250W	
Tumbler, Rare	50						75W	
SUNKEN DAISY (ENGLISH)								
Sugar	30		40					
SUNKEN HOLLYHOCK								
G-W-T-W Lamp, Rare	4,000							12,000
SUNRAY								
Compote		40			55			
SUNRAY (FENTON)								
Compote (Milk Glass Iridized)					90MO			
SUPERB DRAPE (NORTHWOOD)								
Vase, Rare						2,700*		
SWAN, PASTEL (DUGAN-FENTON)								
One Size	225	300	500TL*	190	375		125IG	
SWEETHEART (CAMBRIDGE)								
Cookie Jar w/lid, Rare	1,550		1,100					
Tumbler, Rare	650							
SWALLOWS								
Tumbler, Enameled	120.00							
SWIRL (NORTHWOOD)								
Pitcher	250		800					
Tumbler	110		150					
SWIRL (IMPERIAL)								
Mug, Rare	90							
Candlestick, Each	35							
SWIRL HOBNAIL (MILLERSBURG)								
Rose Bowl, Rare	295	375	650					
Spittoon, Rare	575	750	1,250					
Vase, 7"-10", Rare	250	300	300	500				
SWIRL VARIANT (IMPERIAL)								
Bowl, 7"-8"	30							
Epergne			200		45			
Vase, 6½"	35		45		200		65W	
Plate, 6"-8¾"	50		60		60		75	
Pitcher, 7½"	100							
Cake Plate							85CL	
Dessert, Stemmed	30							
Juice Glass	40							
SWIRLED FLUTE (FENTON)								
Vase, 7"-12"	35	40	50	45			70W	485
SWIRLED RIBS (NORTHWOOD)								
Pitcher	165							
Tumbler	70	75						
SWIRLED THREADS								
Goblet	95							
SWORD AND CIRCLE								
Tumbler, Rare	150							
SYDNEY (FOSTORIA)								
Tumbler, Rare	800							
TAFFETA LUSTRE (FOSTORIA)								
Candlestick, Pair, Rare		300	350	400			450AM	
Console Bowl, 11", Rare		150	150	175			180AM	
(Add 25% For Old Paper Labels Attached)								
Perfume w/stopper	90	125					160LV	
TALL HAT								
Various Sizes, 4"-10"	45+						50PK	
TARGET (FENTON)								
Vase, 7"-11"	45	55	60		95		55	
TEXAS								
Giant Tumbler				260				
TEXAS HEADDRESS (WESTMORELAND)								
Punch Cup	45							

	M	A	G	B	PO	AO	Pas	R
TEN MUMS (FENTON)								
Bowl, Ftd, 9", Rare	500							
Bowl, 8"-11"	95	125	120	150				
Plate, 10", Rare				975				
Pitcher, Rare	495			900			1,500W	
Tumbler, Rare	70			80			340W	
THIN RIB (FENTON)								
Candlestick, Pair	80							390
THIN RIB AND DRAPE (FENTON)								
Vase, 8"-14"	40	50	55					
THIN RIB (NORTHWOOD) AND VTS								
Vase, 6"-11"	35	40	50	55	70	235	70	
THISTLE (ENGLISH)								
Vase, 6"	45							
THISTLE (FENTON)								
Bowl, 8"-10"	90	140	160	150			400AQ	
Plate, 9", Rare		1,650	2,800					
Compote	60			70				
Advertising Bowl (Horlacher)	125	225	200	200				
THISTLE								
Shade	60							
THISTLE AND LOTUS (FENTON)								
Bowl, 7"	55		75	70				
THISTLE AND THORN (ENGLISH)								
Bowl, Ftd, 6"	50							
Creamer or Sugar, Each	60							
Plate, Ftd, 8½"	150							
Nut Bowl	75							
THISTLE, FENTON'S (FENTON)								
Banana Boat, Ftd, Scarce	300	400	500	475				
THREE DIAMONDS (DUGAN)								
Vase, 6"-10"	45	50	60	60	75		60	
THREE FLOWERS (IMPERIAL)								
Tray, Center Handle, 12"	60						70SM	
THREE FRUITS (NORTHWOOD)								
Bowl, 9"	45	90	150	180		750	240	
Bowl, 5"	30	40	70	80		150	70	
Bowl, Dome Base, 8⅝"		90						
Bon-bon, Stemmed	50	65	80	90		850	120	
Plate, Round, 9"	200	400	290	375		2,800	900IB	
(Add 50% if Stippled)								
Bowl, Stippled, 9"	150	250	1,000	395		1,400		
THREE FRUITS MEDALLION (NORTHWOOD)								
Bowl, Ftd, 8-10½", Rare (Meander Exterior)	120	195	240	285		1,400	500AQ	
THREE FRUITS VT. (DUGAN)								
Plate, 12-Sided	150	175	200				160	
THREE-IN-ONE (IMPERIAL)								
Bowl, 8¾"	30	40	40				45SM	
Bowl, 4½"	20	25	25				30SM	
Plate, 6½"	50						80SM	
Rose Bowl, Rare	200							
Banana Bowl Whimsey	100							
Toothpick Holder, Rare			85					
THREE MONKEYS								
Bottle, Rare							90	
THREE ROLL								
Bedroom Set (Tumble Up)	90							
THREE ROW (IMPERIAL)								
Vase, Rare	900	1,200					1,100SM	
THUMBPRINT AND OVAL (IMPERIAL)								
Vase, 5½", Rare	600	850						
THUMBPRINT AND SPEARS								
Creamer	50		60					
THUNDERBIRD (AUSTRALIAN)								
Bowl, 9½"	350	395						
Bowl, 5"	60	75						

Ten Mums

Thin Rib and Drape

Three Fruits

Three-In-One

Tomahawk

Tracery

Tornado

Tree Bark

	M	A	G	B	PO	AO	Pas	R
TIERED THUMBPRINT								
Bowls, 2 Sizes	45							
Candlestick, Pair	120							
TIGER LILY								
(IMPERIAL)								
Pitcher	125	350	275					
Tumbler	35	60	40	350			90AM	
TINY BERRY								
Tumbler, 2¼"			45					
TINY HOBNAIL								
Lamp	110							
TOBACCO LEAF								
(U.S. GLASS)								
Champagne							160CL	
TOLTEC								
(McKEE)								
Butter (Ruby Iridized),								
Rare		375						
Pitcher, Tankard,								
Very Rare	2,600*							
TOMOHAWK								
(CAMBRIDGE)								
One Size, Rare				1,850				
TOP HAT								
Vase							50	
TOP O' THE MORNING								
Hatpin		50						
TOP O' THE WALK								
Hatpin		100						
TORNADO								
(NORTHWOOD)								
Vase, Plain	450	550	500	1,200			1,200W	
Vase, Ribbed, 2 Sizes	495	575	550	1,150			1,500IB	
Vase Whimsey							1,300WS	
TORNADO VT.								
(NORTHWOOD)								
Vase, Rare	1,450							
TOWERS								
(ENGLISH)								
Hat Vase	65							
TOY PUNCH SET								
(CAMBRIDGE)								
Bowl Only, Ftd	60							
TRACERY								
(MILLERSBURG)								
Bon-bon, Rare		650	650					
TREE BARK								
(IMPERIAL)								
Pitcher, Open Top	60							
Pitcher w/lid	70							
Tumbler, 2 Sizes	25							
Bowl, 7½"	20							
Pickle Jar, 7½"	35							
Candlestick, 7", Pair	50							
Sauce, 4"	10							
Candlestick, 4½", Pair	30							
Candy Jar w/lid	35							
TREEBARK VT.								
Candleholder on stand	85							
Pitcher	60							
Tumbler	20							
Planter	60							
Juice	25							
TREE OF LIFE								
(IMPERIAL)								
Bowl, 5½"	30							
Handled Basket	30							
Plate, 7½"	40							
Tumbler	25							
Pitcher	60							
Perfumer w/lid	40							
Vase Whimsey (From Pitcher)..						150CL		
TREE TRUNK								
(NORTHWOOD)								
Vase, 7"-12"	75	150	95	100		1,200	250IB	
Funeral Vase, 15"-20"	950	1,500	1,250	1,400	2,800*MO	6,500	6,000IG	
Jardinere Whimsey, Rare	2,000	2,500						
TREFOIL FINE CUT								
(MILLERSBURG)								
Exterior pattern only								
TRIAD								
Hatpin		55						
TRIANDS								
(ENGLISH)								
Creamer, Sugar or Spooner	50							
Butter	65							
Celery Vase	55							

Tulip and Cane

Twins

Two Flowers

	M	A	G	B	PO	AO	Pas	R
TRIPLETS (DUGAN)								
Bowl, 6"-8"	35	40	45		55			
Hat	30	35	38					
TROPICANA (ENGLISH)								
Vase, Rare	1,600							
TROUT AND FLY (MILLERSBURG)								
Bowl, 8¾", Various Shapes	500	600	750				1,100LV	
Plate, 9", Rare		7,500						
TULIP (MILLERSBURG)								
Compote, 9", Rare	750	850	800					
TULIP AND CANE (IMPERIAL)								
Wine, 2 Sizes, Rare	85							
Claret Goblet, Rare	110							
Goblet, 8 oz, Rare	75							
Compote	45							
TULIP SCROLL (MILLERSBURG)								
Vase, 6"-12", Rare	275	400	300					
TUMBLE-UP (FENTON-IMPERIAL)								
Plain, Complete	85						90	
Handled, Complete, Rare	295						320	
TWINS (IMPERIAL)								
Bowl, 9"	40		50				45	
Bowl, 5"	25		30				35	
Fruit Bowl w/base	60							
TWITCH (BARTLETT-COLLINS)								
Cup	30							
Creamer	30							
Sherbet	35							
TWO FLOWERS (FENTON)								
Plate, 13", Rare	1,100							7,000
Bowl, Ftd, 5"-8"	60	70	70	55				
Bowl, Spatula, 8"	90	110	135	120			250W	2,200
Rose Bowl, Rare	195		225	200				
Bowl, Ftd, 8"-10"	75	175	250	275			375W	5,800
Plate, Ftd, 9"	600		675	650				
TWO FRUITS (FENTON)								
Divided Bowl, 5½" Scarce	75	90	115	95			120W	
TWO ROW (IMPERIAL)								
Vase, Rare		1,100						
URN								
Vase, 9"	65							
US DIAMOND BLOCK (U.S. GLASS)								
Compote, Rare	65				90			
Shakers, Pair	80							
UMBRELLA PRISMS								
Small Hatpin		45						
Large Hatpin		70						
UNIVERSAL HOME BOTTLE								
One Shape	125*							
UNSHOD								
Pitcher	85							
UTILITY								
Lamp, 8", Complete	90							
VALENTINE								
Ring Tray	80							
VALENTINE (NORTHWOOD)								
Bowl, 10", Rare	500							
Bowl, 5", Rare	125	200						
474 VARIANT (SWEDEN)								
Compote, 7"			90					
VENETIAN (CAMBRIDGE)								
Vase, (Lamp Base), 9¼", Rare	1,500		1,300					
Creamer, Rare	550							
Sugar, Rare	550							
Butter, Rare	950							

Two Fruits

	M	A	G	B	PO	AO	Pas	R
VICTORIAN								
Bowl, 10"-12", Rare		500			2,500			
VINEYARD (DUGAN)								
Pitcher..............................	90	300			950			
Tumbler	25	50					300W	
VINEYARD AND FISHNET (IMPERIAL)								
Vase, Rare								750
VINEYARD HARVEST (AUSTRALIAN)								
Tumbler, Rare	250							
VINING LEAF AND VT. (ENGLISH)								
Spittoon, Rare	350							
Vase, Rare	225							
Rose Bowl, Rare	250							
VINING TWIGS (DUGAN)								
Bowl, 7½"	35	45	50				55	
Hat......................................	40	50					60W	
VINTAGE (FENTON)								
Epergne, One Lily, 2 Sizes ...	100	135	150	150			200AM	980
Fernery, 2 Varieties	55	70	100	95			85	4,800
Bowl, 10"............................	45	60	90	125			70	3,600
Bowl, 8"..............................	40	45	50	50		1,000	60	2,500
Bowl, 6½"	30	40	45	45			55	
Bowl, 4½"	25	35	40	40			45	
Plate, 7¾"	280	185	200	130				
Whimsey Fernery.................		200						
Card Tray	40							
Punch Bowl w/base.............	275	400	450	465				
(Wreath of Roses Exterior)								
Cup.....................................	25	35	37	40				
Rose Bowl............................	55			60				
Compote..............................	40	50	55	60				
Plate, 7"	115			240				
Plate, Ruffled, 11"................	200		275	295				
VINTAGE (DUGAN)								
Powder Jar w/lid	70	120		150				
Dresser Tray, 7" x 11"..........	85							
VINTAGE (U.S. GLASS)								
Wine....................................	40	50						
VINTAGE (MILLERSBURG)								
Bowl, 5", Rare.....................	500		600	800				
Bowl, 9", Rare.....................	600	900	800	3,500				
VINTAGE BANDED (DUGAN)								
Mug.....................................	35						45SM	
Tumbler, Rare	600							
Pitcher................................	250	550						
VINTAGE LEAF (FENTON)								
Bowl, 8½"	50	75	85	70				
Bowl, 5½"	25	35	40	30				
VINTAGE VT. (DUGAN)								
Plate....................................	300	400						
Bowl, Ftd, 8½"			100				450WS	
VIOLET								
Basket, Either Type	50	65		75				
VIRGINIA BLACKBERRY (U.S. GLASS)								
Pitcher, Small, Rare.............				250				
(Note: Tiny Berry Miniature Tumbler May Match This.)								
VOTIVE LIGHT (MEXICAN)								
Candle Vase, 4½", Rare	450							
WAFFLE BLOCK (IMPERIAL)								
Handled Basket, 10"	50						165TL	
Bowl, 7"-9"	40							
Parfait Glass, Stemmed	30						45	
Fruit Bowl w/base..............							200CM	
Vase, 8"-11"..........................	40						55	
Nappy..................................							40PM	
Pitcher................................	120						170CM	
Tumbler	200						215CM	
Rose Bowl, Any Size.............	70							
Plate, 10"-12", Any Shape	85						170SM	
Sherbet							35CL	
Punch Bowl	175						225TL	
Cup.....................................	20						30TL	
Shakers, Pair......................	75							
Creamer	60							
Sugar	60							

Vineyard

Wheat

Vintage Banded

Votive Light

	M	A	G	B	PO	AO	Pas	R
WAFFLE BLOCK AND HOBSTAR (IMPERIAL)								
Basket	250						265SM	
WAFFLE WEAVE								
Inkwell	95							
WAR DANCE (ENGLISH)								
Compote, 5"	120							
WASHBOARD								
Creamer, 5½"	45							
WATER LILY (FENTON)								
Bon-bon	40	50	55	50			60	
Bowl, Ftd, 5"	50	90	300	100			150V	1,600
Bowl, Ftd, 10"	90	140	400	250			175BA	3,700
Chop Plate 11", Very Rare	4,500*							
WATER LILY AND CATTAILS (FENTON)								
Toothpick Whimsey	75							
Bon-bon	60	85		90				
Pitcher	340							
Tumbler	95							
Butter	175							
Sugar	100							
Creamer or Spooner	75							
Bowl, 5"	35	50		50				
Bowl, 7"-9"	50							
Spittoon Whimsey, Rare	2,400							
WATER LILY AND CATTAILS (NORTHWOOD)								
Pitcher	400			6,000				
Tumbler	110	200		2,700*				
WATER LILY AND DRAGONFLY (AUSTRALIAN)								
Float Bowl, 10½", Complete	150	185						
WAVEY SATIN								
Hatpin		95						
WEBBED CLEMATIS								
Vase, 12½"	250							
WEEPING CHERRY (DUGAN)								
Bowl, Dome Base	90	130			220		100	
Bowl, Flat Base	75	110			190		90	
WESTERN DAISY (WESTMORELAND)								
Bowl		50	60		200MO			
Hat		45	50					
WESTERN THISTLE								
Tumbler, Rare	340							
Vase. Rare	250							
WESTMORELAND JESTER'S CAP								
Vase	40	50	55	60	75	225	85	
WHEAT (NORTHWOOD)								
Sweetmeat w/lid, Rare		9,000	9,500					
Bowl w/lid, Rare		8,000						
WHEELS (IMPERIAL)								
Bowl, 9"	50							
WHIRLING HOBSTAR (U.S. GLASS)								
Punch Bowl w/base	125							
Cup	20							
Pitcher	190							
WHIRLING LEAVES (MILLERSBURG)								
Bowl, 9"-11", Round or Ruffled	95	400	450				250CM	
Bowl, 10", Tri-Cornered	300	500	500				550V	
WHIRLING STAR (IMPERIAL)								
Bowl, 9"-11"	40							
Compote	55		85					
Punch Bowl w/base	135							
Cup	20							
WHITE ELEPHANT								
Ornament, Rare							350W	
WHITE OAK								
Tumbler, Rare	300							
WICKERWORK (ENGLISH)								
Bowl w/base, Complete	275							
WIDE PANEL (U.S. GLASS)								
Salt	50							

Waterlily and Cattails

Water Lily and Dragonfly

Webbed Clematis

Whirling Leaves

Wide Rib Vase

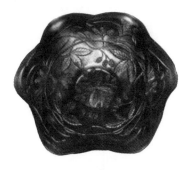

Wild Blackberry

Wildflower (Northwood)

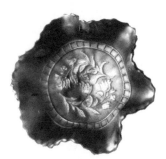

Wildflower

	M	A	G	B	PO	AO	Pas	R
WIDE PANEL (NORTHWOOD-FENTON-IMPERIAL)								
Bowl, 9"	45	90					80SM	
Compote	40							
Epergne, 4 Lily, Rare	1,000	1,600	1,700	2,000		28,000	1,900W	
Console Set, 3 Pieces	110						135	
Goblet	40							290
Cake Plate, 12"-15", Rare	150UP	250UP					270UP	400
Punch Bowl	115							1,175
Cup	20							150
Lemonade, Handled	30						75W	
Compote, Miniature	40							
Covered Candy	40	60						390
Spittoon Whimsey	500							
Vase	30	40	45	60			70	700
WIDE PANEL (WESTMORELAND)								
Bowl, 7½"							70TL	
Bowl, 8¼"							75TL	
WIDE PANEL BOUQUET								
Basket, 3½"	75							
WIDE PANEL SHADE								
Lightshade			175					
WIDE PANEL VT. (NORTHWOOD)								
Pitcher, Tankard	200	275	300					
WIDE RIB (DUGAN)								
Vase	55	60	70	70	90	300	85	
WILD BERRY								
Jar w/lid	250							
WILD BLACKBERRY (FENTON)								
Bowl, 8½", Scarce	65	90	110					
Bowl, "Maday" Advertising, Rare		1,250*	1,500*					
WILD FERN (AUSTRALIAN)								
Compote	165	240						
WILDFLOWER (MILLERSBURG)								
Compote, Ruffled, Rare	1,000	1,200	1,500					
Compote, Jelly, Rare		1,600						
WILDFLOWER (NORTHWOOD)								
Compote (Plain Interior)	300	350	350					
WILD GRAPE								
Bowl, 8¾"	60							
WILD LOGANBERRY (WESTMORELAND)								
Cider Pitcher, Rare							520IM	
Compote, Covered, Rare							295IM	
Creamer, Rare							150IM	
Sugar, Rare							100IM	
Wine	145							
Goblet					150			
(Note: Also Known as Dewberry)								
WILD ROSE (NORTHWOOD)								
Bowl, Flat, 8"	40	50	45					
Bowl, Ftd, Open Edge, 6"	45	65	75				150BA	
WILD ROSE (MILLERSBURG)								
Small Lamp, Rare	1,000	1,200	1,100					
Medium Lamp, Rare	1,200	1,500	1,200					
Lamp, Marked "Riverside," Very Rare			3,000*					
Medallion Lamp, Rare	2,000	2,500	2,300					
WILD ROSE								
Syrup, Rare	700							
WILD ROSE SHADE								
Lightshade	95							
WILD STRAWBERRY (DUGAN)								
Bowl, 9"-10½"	200	300	300		375			
Plate, 7"-9", Rare		375						
Bowl, 6", Rare	60	95			140			
WINDFLOWER (DUGAN)								
Bowl, 8½"	95			85				
Plate, 9"	165			160				
Nappy, Handled	85	95		185			95PK	
WINDMILL (IMPERIAL)								
Bowl, 9"	35	40	40				140V	
Bowl, 5"	20	25	25					
Fruit Bowl, 10½"	40		40					
Milk Pitcher	60	170	110					
Pickle Dish	25		45					
Tray, Flat	35		65				80	
Pitcher	70	200	160				425	
Tumbler	25	95	45				175AM	
WINDSOR (IMPERIAL)								
Flower Arranger, Rare	90						90IB	

Wishbone Flower Arranger

Woodlands Vase

Wreath of Roses Variant

Zig-Zag

	M	A	G	B	PO	AO	Pas	R
WINE AND ROSES (FENTON)								
Cider Pitcher, Scarce	665							
Wine............................	90			95		550	120AO	
WINGED HEAVY SHELL								
Vase, 3½".............................							95	
WINKEN								
Lamp............................	135							
WISE OWL								
Bank	50							
WISHBONE (IMPERIAL)								
Flower Arranger..................	90						90	
WISHBONE (NORTHWOOD)								
Bowl, Flat, 8"-10"	190	150	160	370			900IB	
Bowl, Ftd, 9".....................	200	170	190				1,300SM	
Epergne, Rare.....................	400	550	850				1,700W	
Plate, Ftd, 9", Rare	900	400						
Plate, Flat, 10", Rare...........	500	875	900					
Pitcher, Rare.....................	800	1,000	990					
Tumbler, Scarce	95	170	200				400PL	
WISHBONE AND SPADES (DUGAN)								
Bowl, 8½"		395			200			
Bowl, 5"..............................		250			190			
Plate, 6", Rare.....................		395			300			
Plate, 10½", Rare		1,100			1,350			
WISTERIA (NORTHWOOD)								
Bank Whimsey, Rare							2,500W	
Pitcher, Rare.....................							7,500IB	
Tumbler, Rare							900IB	
WITCHES POT								
One Shape, Souvenir...........	850							
WOODEN SHOE								
One Shape, Rare	275							
WOODLANDS								
Vase, 5", Rare	300							
WOODPECKER (DUGAN)								
Wall Vase............................	55		90				115V	
WOODPECKER AND IVY								
Vase, Rare			1,900				2,100V	
WREATH OF ROSES (FENTON)								
Bon-bon	40	45	50	45			65	
Bon-bon, Stemmed..............	45	50	50	50			65	
Compote.............................	45	50	50	45				
Punch Bowl w/base.............	2,000	350	375	390	2,000			
Cup...................................	25	30	35	40	320			
WREATH OF ROSES VT. (DUGAN)								
Compote.............................	55	65	65	60				
WREATHED BLEEDING HEARTS (DUGAN)								
Vase, 5¼"............................	110							
WREATHED CHERRY (DUGAN)								
Oval Bowl, 10½"...................	90	140		300			225W	
Oval Bowl, 5".......................	40	40		75			60W	
Butter	110	160					195W	
Sugar	70	100					110W	
Creamer or Spooner	65	95					100W	
Toothpick, Old Only............		175						
Pitcher...............................	240	425					775W	
Tumbler	40	55					170W	
ZIG ZAG (FENTON)								
Pitcher, Decorated, Rare	250			450			575IG	
Tumbler, Decorated	40			50			75IG	
ZIG ZAG (MILLERSBURG)								
Bowl, Round or Ruffled, 9½" ...	275	350	375					
Bowl, Tri-Cornered, 10".......	450	575	575					
Card Tray, Rare...................			900					
ZIPPER LOOP (IMPERIAL)								
Hand Lamp, Rare	1,300						1,500SM	
Medium Lamp, Rare	600						600SM	
Large Lamp, Rare	500						500SM	
ZIPPER STITCH (CZECH)								
Cordial Set (Tray, Decanter, 4 Cordials), Complete	1,700							
ZIPPER VT. (ENGLISH)								
Sugar w/lid	50							
ZIPPERED HEART								
Bowl, 9".............................	70	110						
Bowl, 5".............................	40	50						
Queen's Vase, Rare..............	4,000	3,800						
Pitcher (Not Confirmed)	1,000*	1,500*						
Tumbler (Not Confirmed)	120*	150*						
ZIP ZIP (ENGLISH)								
Flower Frog Holder	60							

Schroeder's
ANTIQUES
Price Guide

. . . is the #1 best-selling antiques & collectibles value guide on the market today, and here's why . . .

Identification & Values Of Over 50,000 Antiques & Collectibles

8½ x 11, 608 Pages, $14.95

• *More than 300 advisors, well-known dealers, and top-notch collectors work together with our editors to bring you accurate information regarding pricing and identification.*

• *More than 45,000 items in almost 500 categories are listed along with hundreds of sharp original photos that illustrate not only the rare and unusual, but the common, popular collectibles as well.*

• *Each large close-up shot shows important details clearly. Every subject is represented with histories and background information, a feature not found in any of our competitors' publications.*

• *Our editors keep abreast of newly developing trends, often adding several new categories a year as the need arises.*

If it merits the interest of today's collector, you'll find it in Schroeder's. And you can feel confident that the information we publish is up to date and accurate. Our advisors thoroughly check each category to spot inconsistencies, listings that may not be entirely reflective of market dealings, and lines too vague to be of merit. Only the best of the lot remains for publication.

Without doubt, you'll find
SCHROEDER'S ANTIQUES PRICE GUIDE
the only one to buy for
reliable information and values.

COLLECTOR BOOKS
A Division of Schroeder Publishing Co., Inc.